ANIMAL DRAWING
AND ANATOMY

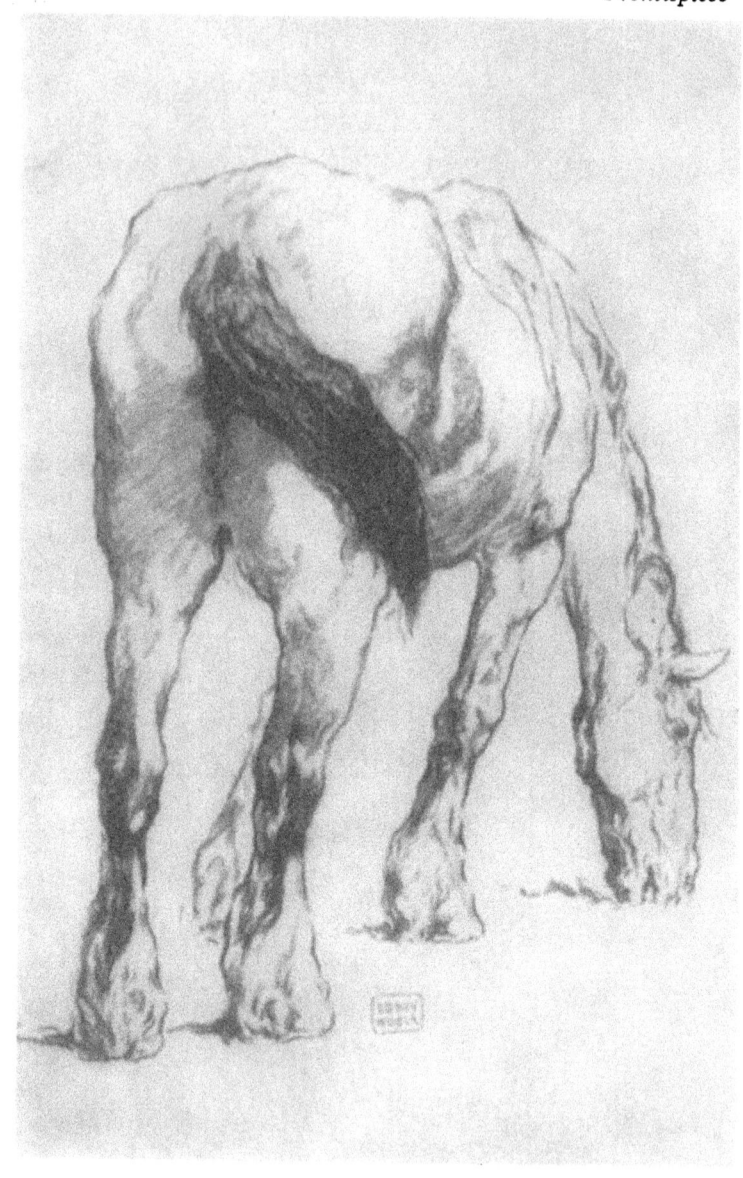

HORSE GRAZING

ANIMAL DRAWING AND ANATOMY

EDWIN NOBLE

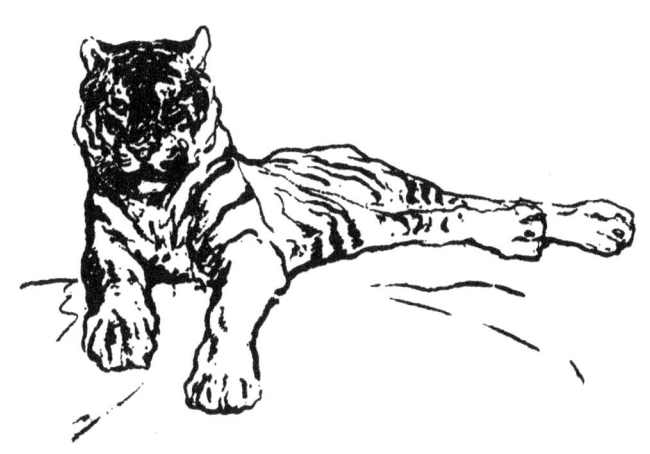

DOVER PUBLICATIONS, INC.
Mineola, New York

Bibliographical Note

This Dover edition, first published in 2002, is an unabridged, unaltered repub-
lication of the text and illustrations from the work originally published in 1928
by B. T. Batsford, Ltd., London.

Library of Congress Cataloging-in-Publication Data

Noble, Edwin, 1876–1941.
    Animal drawing and anatomy / Edwin Noble.
        p. cm.
    Originally published: London : Batsford, 1928.
    Includes index.
    ISBN-13: 978-0-486-42312-8 (pbk.)
    ISBN-10: 0-486-42312-3 (pbk.)
      1. Animals in art. 2. Anatomy, Artistic. 3. Drawing—Technique. I. Title.

NC780 .N6 2002
743.6—dc21

2002067288

www.doverpublications.com

PREFACE

NO artist, designer, or craftsman can be regarded as fully equipped without a knowledge of natural forms. All forms of life offer rich material for design, whether realistic or conventional. Study from the life, of the human figure, the forms of all animals and birds, and of the inhabitants of the waters, and of plants, must precede mastery of the art of design.

For that reason this book should be welcome to all students of art. While it is usual to teach drawing from the human figure and the study of plant forms, the decorative material provided by the forms of animals and birds has been almost entirely neglected. This book, therefore, is most opportune, coming as it does at a time when a little more interest is being shown.

After all, the study of animal and bird forms is right in the main stream of artistic tradition. The early sculptors made great use of this material, although rather naively at times. We find animals and birds often represented in the decoration of many of the buildings of the past, in mediaeval churches, and in heraldry, tapestry, and all forms of painting and decoration.

Nature is the mistress of decoration, and all who would understand it must sit at her feet. To the essential study of the clearly-defined law of pattern in Nature this book makes an important contribution.

Frank Brangwyn.

October 1928.

INTRODUCTION

A QUICK eye and unlimited patience are the great essentials for successful delineation of living birds and animals. When speaking of patience, I do not mean that which can only slavishly copy intricate details, but the patience which can afford to await opportunity. The figure painter may pose his models, but the animal painter can only snatch his opportunities. His model may remain still for half an hour, or half a minute; the latter is the amount of time most probable and all that he should allow himself, and in that short period he must make all his notes.

The drawing of animals whilst in the act of movement requires considerable skill and experience, and it is inadvisable to attempt this at too early a stage. The most satisfactory method is to wait for such momentary pauses as occur in attitudes of watching, listening or feeding, and, above all, every advantage taken of sleeping and sitting positions. These often show some exceptional foreshortening, and the knowledge so gained can be applied in future drawings wherein action is depicted. Whatever the position may be, however, every opportunity should be taken of the involuntary movements denoting the presence of life. It may be only the twitching of the tail tip, or angle of ears, but by their introduction is avoided all appearance of a dead or stuffed animal.

The simplest and most direct method of drawing should be cultivated from the commencement, the uncertainty of how long the model will retain the pose being sufficient to demonstrate the importance of this fact. A treatment so

INTRODUCTION

often advocated in other branches of art, namely, that of getting a general effect first, and adding details afterwards, is usually fatal to the student of animal drawing. In the event of change of position the sketch, however slight, should be complete in itself, with correctly suggested details of eyes, ears, or feet. Should the opportunity present itself of continued work upon the drawing, one can proceed with further elaboration.

Owing to the danger of getting two or more positions into one outline, it is inadvisable to attempt big alterations, but rather to commence a fresh drawing entirely.

A certain knowledge of the anatomy and characteristics of the various animals is also essential from the commencement. Hair requires to be treated as something of more importance to the visible form than can be suggested by a few haphazard scratches reminiscent of grass or cotton-wool, and the detail of the overlapping of feathers should be studied from the dead or stuffed model before proceeding far with sketches from life. Models for this purpose can often be purchased from the local poulterer; Pigeons, Pheasants, Guinea Fowl, Wild Duck, Hares, etc., making excellent material, and by the aid of skewers, pins, and cotton may be arranged in life-like positions of walking or flying.

Cultivation of the memory is a most important attribute, the mental visualization of a phase of action being indispensable, and, finally, every opportunity should be taken to make quick colour notes of the effect of light and sunshine upon plumage or the sheen of the coat.

Edwin Noble, *F.Z.S.*

October, 1928.

CONTENTS

xi

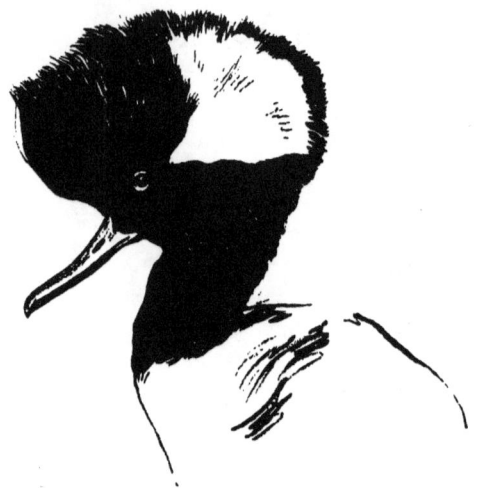

HOODED MERGANSER DUCK

CHAPTER I

SHEEP

A S a model, the domestic sheep has always been of interest to the artist. Its stereotyped movements, constantly repeated by dozens of companions in its immediate vicinity, should logically mean an easy animal to study, whereas the contrary is the case and capable draughtsmen and painters when making such sketches find them most baffling, owing to the lack of any salient points to seize upon. This, however, is largely due to their own lack of knowledge of the one great important fact —namely, the Anatomy of the Wool.

A general impression exists that feathers and hair grow from the body in a manner similar to that of the bristles from a door-mat. If that were so, we should expect to find a wrinkling of the feathers similar to that of the human skin becoming apparent at every point of movement during violent action. This, however, does not occur owing to the feathers themselves passing one above another by a telescopic or fanlike movement, laying closely over-lapped upon the inner side and upon the outer side allowing a larger portion of each feather to be visible. On this account undue exposure of flesh is seldom noticeable in birds, but in the case of animals it is often more apparent.

Very few animals are without a coat or hairy covering in some form or another, and in most cases this has two characteristics—namely, a woolly undergrowth close to the skin for the purpose of warmth, and an outer covering or thatch, of long and usually straight hairs, for protection against weather.

PLATE I

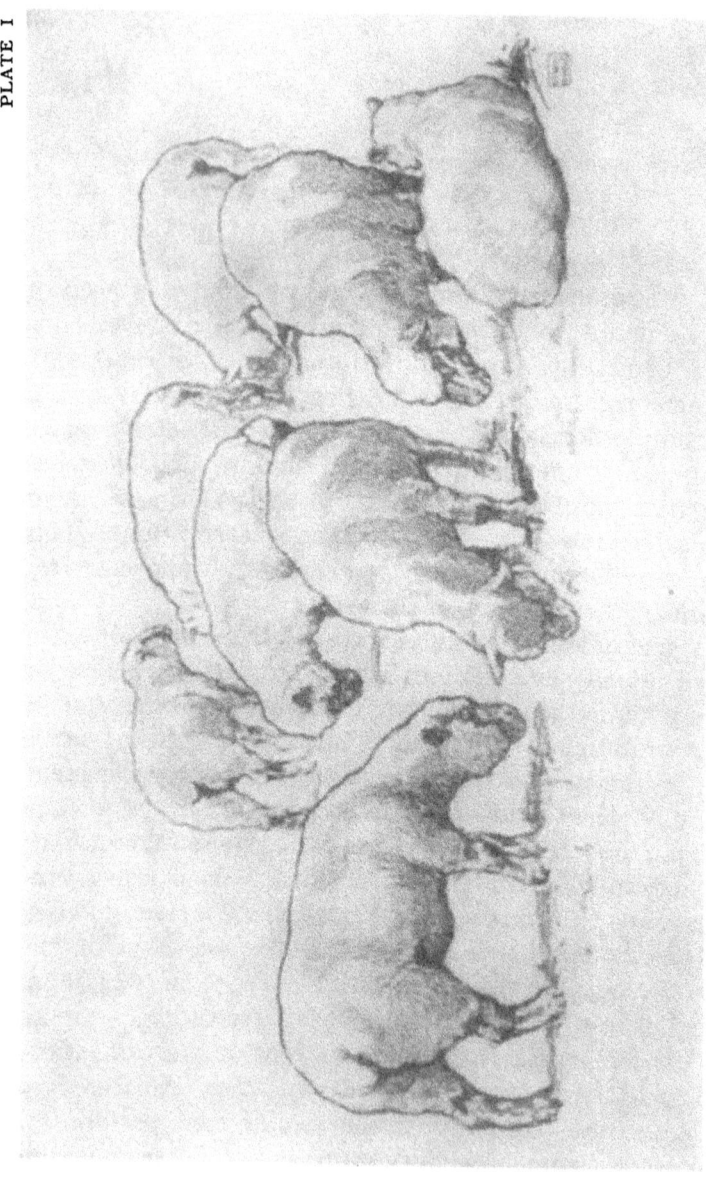

SHEEP

SHOWING THE GENERAL DIRECTION OF THE CRACKING OF THE WOOL

The latter usually predominates upon the upper parts of the body, and in most cases at the angles of limbs, etc., serving the purpose of a gutter to run away the rain or prevent it settling upon the under side of the body where the more delicate organs are situated. Wool serves better than hair for such portions of the body whereon the skin has excessive play due to the movements of the limb beneath, and consequently distinct areas of wool may be found which appear to crack open when the skin is thus extended. This peculiarity is of great importance from the picturesque point of view, inasmuch as it ceases to exist after the death of the animal, with the result that the slightest of notes from the living model will give something never found in the stuffed specimen. The movements of the head, for example, may be very slight, so much so as to be almost unrecognisable by change in the contour, but this break in the regularity of the hair gives just the amount of emphasis necessary to show the action.

In the domestic sheep the wool has been more or less artificially developed to produce as far as possible an equal quantity all over the body, and the result is a packing of the masses at the points of movement, whilst equal masses betray no movement whatever at points less in action. These latter masses being thus more lethargic are at once seized upon by the inexperienced draughtsman, with the result that unimportant masses are drawn and essentials neglected, and the drawing is a wooden, toy-like sheep without action or life.

Observe the manner in which the neck falls away from the shoulders (Plate ii). In very few animals does this occur in so marked a manner, the general rule being for it to take a slight convex form, due to the heavy muscles which support the head. A ewe neck is a term of disparagement often used to denote a similar formation in a horse or dog, with its consequent loss of strength and beauty.

PLATE II

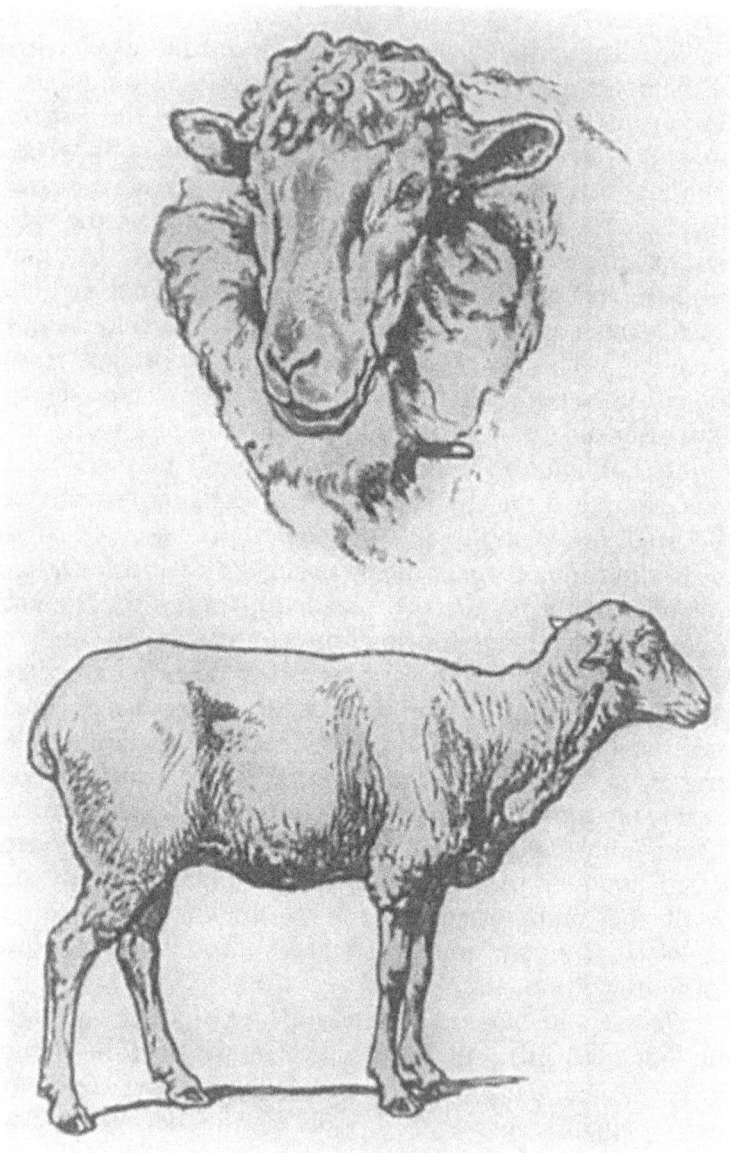

HEAD OF SHEEP
SHOWING ARRANGEMENT OF WOOL

SHOWING THE GENERAL FORMATION OF THE BODY OF A SHEEP BENEATH THE
WOOL COVERING AFTER CLIPPING

4

Careful study of Plate II will show how high the elbow and hind limbs are set upon the body, with its resultant cracking of the wool at these parts. Comparison should be made on these points between the domestic sheep and wild sheep and goats, whereby the symmetry of Nature has been altered with consequent deterioration of stamina. The domestic sheep is unable to travel either far or fast, whilst the wool is unable to stand continuous rain through the loss of the outer coat of long hairs.

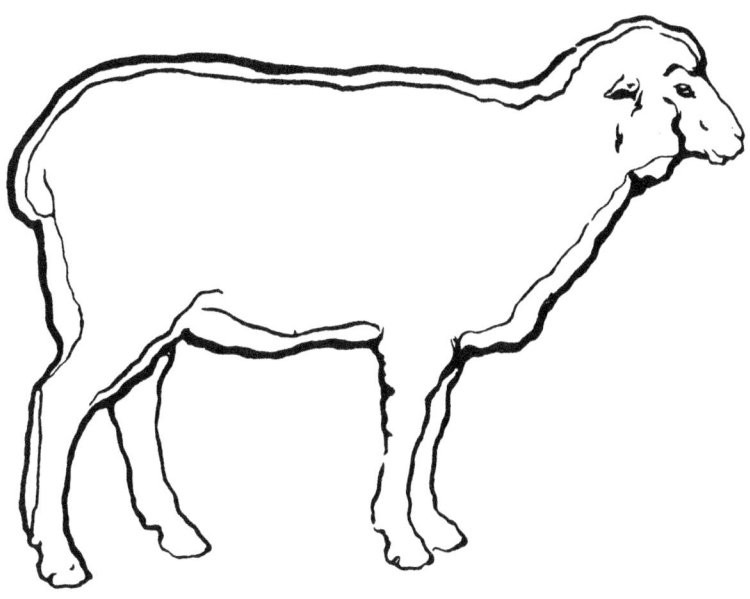

Fig. 1

SHOWING DIFFERENCE OF OUTLINE BETWEEN THE WOOL AND THE BODY OF A SHEEP

PLATE III

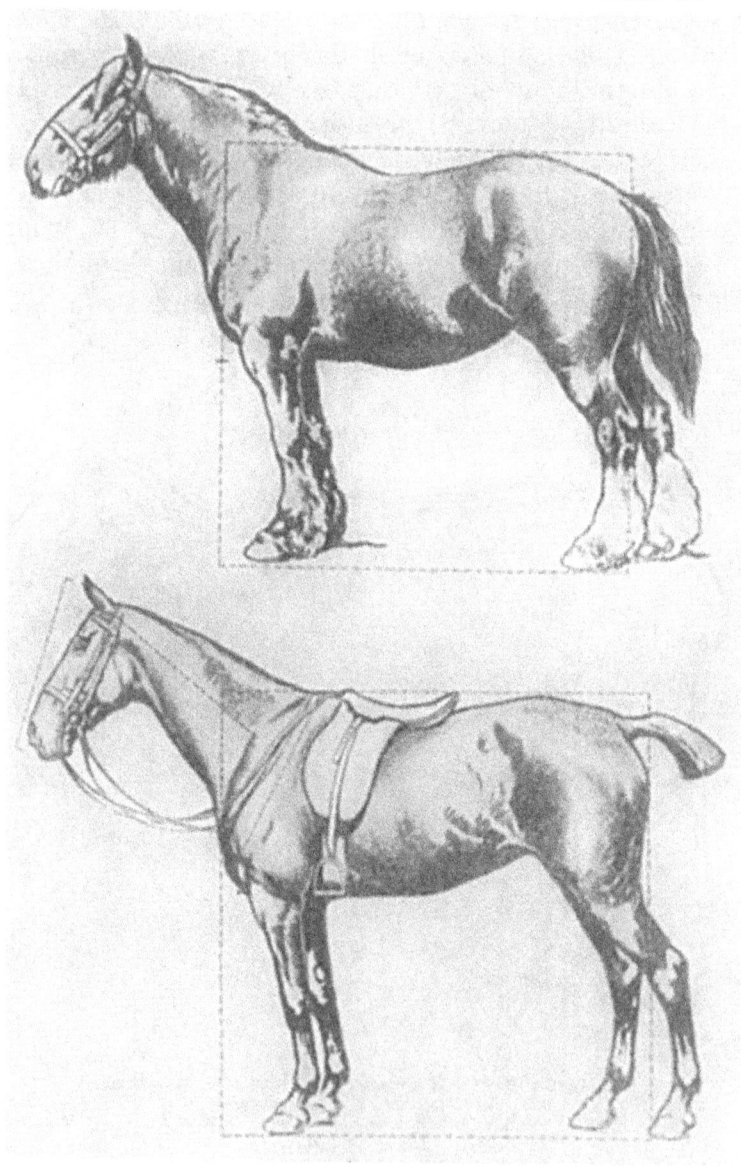

HORSES
SHOWING THE RELATIVE PROPORTIONS OF A HUNTER AND A
HEAVY DRAUGHT HORSE

CHAPTER II

THE HORSE

WHEN dealing with all the domesticated animals, consideration should be given to their present-day artificial conditions of life and interbreeding for special requirements, such as flesh for food, speed, or strength, quantity of coat, etc. In other words, a knowledge of the common ancestor is essential, and provided one can visualise this correctly, the divergence from type can be easily traced, and the character at once seized upon. For example, the bones of a horse's leg become simple to understand if one realises that originally it was of a five-toed animal, about the size of a fox, and known as the *Hyracotherium* (Fig. 2). During the progress of time he grew in size, but lost the use of two of his toes, and the next link comes in the shape of *Mesohippus* (Fig. 3), a three-toed horse with first and fifth toes present, but barely reaching the ground.

From this we come down to the comparatively modern *Hipparion* (Fig. 4), which inhabited these islands previous to man, and excellent fossils are to be found in the Natural History Museum at South Kensington of the bones of the leg and head of this animal.

Living types are found in the Tapir and the Rhinoceros, both closely allied to the Horse tribe. Observe the identical action of their muzzles with that of the upper lip of a Horse when searching for small particles of foods. Both eye and ear are again similar, and the feet of the Tapir show four distinct toes to each front leg and three to each hind

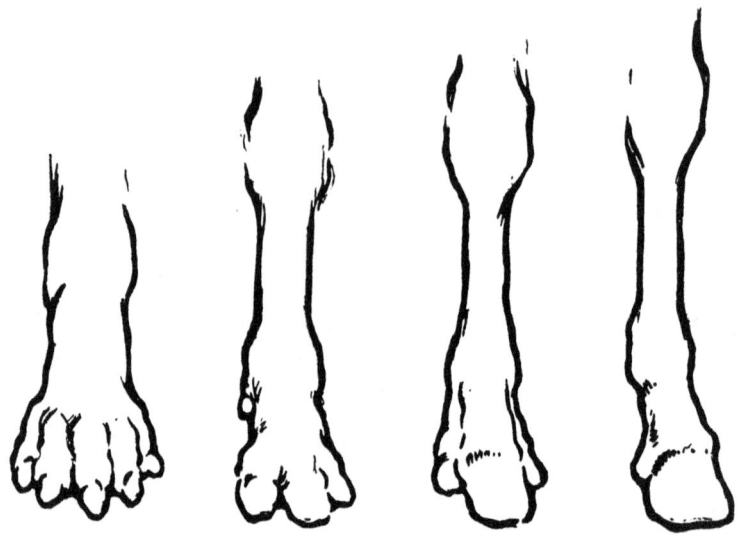

HYPOTHETICAL EVOLUTION OF THE HORSE'S LEG

| FIG. 2. | FIG. 3. | FIG. 4. | FIG. 5. |
| HYRACOTHERIUM | MESOHIPPUS | HIPPARION | HORSE |

leg (Fig. 6), which it has retained in its environment of marshy swamps. Scientific theory is that some forms of this animal left the low-lying swamps and gained an existence in higher and firmer grounds, wherein the soft splay foot not only ceased to become a support, but actually a hindrance to sustained or quick movement. Figs. 2 to 6 show plainly the hypothetical process of evolution and how the middle finger nail finally becomes converted into hoof. The horse still is a three-toed animal, for the splint bones are merely relics of the second and fourth toes in the last stages of their disuse.

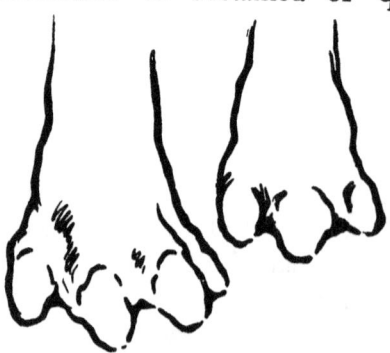

FIG. 6.
FORE AND HIND FOOT OF TAPIR

Another point of interest is the evolution of the tail of a Horse which explains certain characteristics in early sculptures and drawings. Figs. 7 to 10 show the tail of common *Donkey, Zebra, Prjevalski's Horse of Siberia,* and domestic *Horse.* Prjevalski's Horse is believed to be a living type of the original wild horse of Europe, and we find the exact

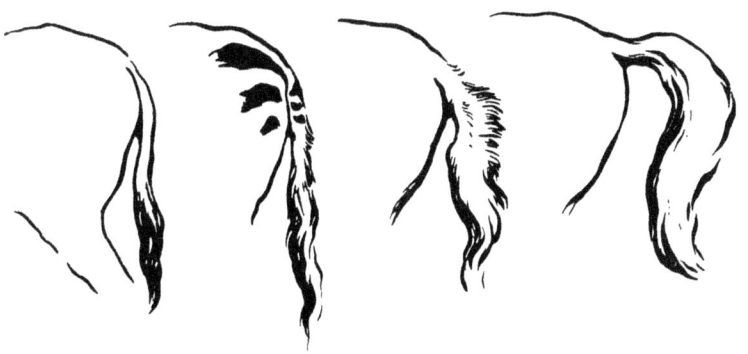

EVOLUTION OF THE HORSE'S TAIL

FIG. 7.	FIG. 8.	FIG. 9.	FIG. 10.
DONKEY	ZEBRA	PRJEVALSKI'S HORSE OF SIBERIA	DOMESTIC HORSE

type of tail which is depicted on all drawings of horses by prehistoric man in France. It is also quite typical of many of the coarser and underbred horses which may be found in Northern Europe to-day, but not that of the Southern parts where the influence of the Barb or Arabian Horse is greater. The tail of the Arab is set on the body in such a way that the spinal column is continued a few inches in a horizontal direction before slowly and gracefully curving downwards, whilst the long plumes of hair commence at the root.

Our race of English Thoroughbreds are descendants from an early Arabian ancestor, and consequently all carry the plumed tail in contrast to that of the English Shire Horse, or Cart Horse, where the tail is curved immediately upon leaving the body, and has a series of short stiffer hairs

ARABIAN THOROUGHBRED   PLATE IV

HEAVY DRAUGHT HORSE

ENGLISH THOROUGHBRED

TYPES OF HORSES AS SHOWN BY SKULLS

upon upper part, and plumed upon lower portion only, a similar type well shown on vases and ornaments of Early Greek Art.

Upon the Parthenon Frieze will be found the Hog Mane of the Prjevalski Horse, and the Ass tribe.

For all ordinary purposes of proportion, the following simple measurements will be sufficient.

A well-bred Hunter (Plate III) or Polo Pony should stand in a square. A line drawn from top of withers to ground should equal one drawn from point of shoulder to point of rump.

The elbow should be exactly half way.

The length of head should equal length of neck from root of ear to shoulder, or length of shoulder from withers to point of shoulder.

The height of a horse is about two and half times the length of head.

In other types of horses, however, these measurements slightly vary. The Thoroughbred Racehorse may stand higher at the withers, due to increased length of leg, although this may be again counteracted by greater slope of shoulder and length of quarters, and the head may be longer. The difference is actually slighter than it appears, and the same applies to the Cart Horse (Plate III). The ideal type should look long and low, and is due to increased depth of ribs; elbow set slightly lower, so shortening and strengthening the legs ; thickening of neck, especially at the base, and so developing chest muscles ; and thickening of the head and jaw.

Both this breed and the Race Horse are specialized types for excessive but short bursts of speed, or strength combined with weight, but the Hunter is the natural combination of both, and conforms to the same standard measurements which apply to other animals requiring similar qualities, notably, the Greyhound and some of the Deer tribe.

PLATE V

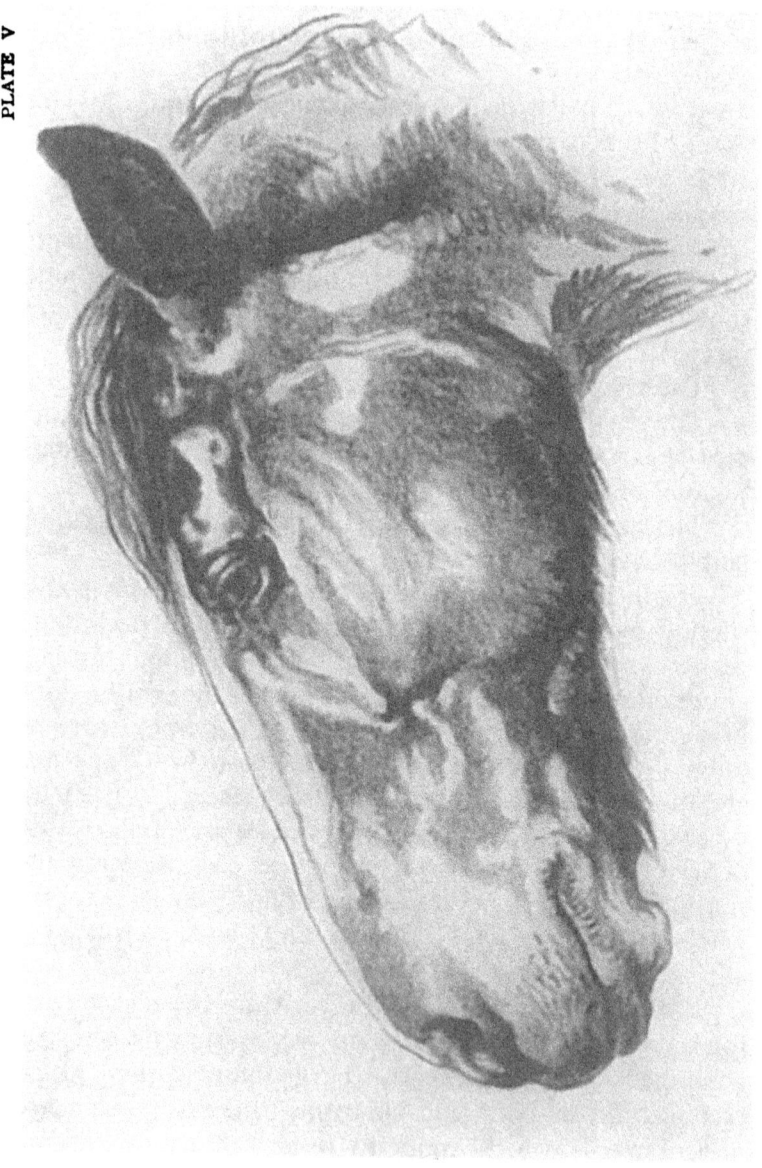

In human portraiture the expression of the sitter lies very largely in the eyes and mouth, but in animal portraiture this is not the case. Very little expression is shown in the eyes of a horse beyond the extremes of fear or anger, and none whatever is shown in the mouth. Ears play a far more important part in expression, the prick forward or otherwise giving some indication of their feelings.

The individual character of every horse is, however, shown to a very marked degree at one point—namely, the contour of the frontal bone.

Plate IV clearly shows the concave contour of the Arabian as compared to the more convex or roman-nosed form of the Cart Horse, whilst the thoroughbred Racehorse is a modified form of both. This can be more easily realized if a tracing be made over each skull. In the foreshortened view this is even more apparent, and in portraiture should always be carefully studied.

A criticism from the owner will often be to the effect that the head is too heavy, and a careful revision of this line will nearly always rectify the fault.

It is a curious point how seldom either owner, trainer, or groom can point out exactly where the portrait fails. They will remark at once whether the likeness is good or otherwise, but words fail them to indicate the precise variation. The explanation is perhaps that they, by continual knowledge of horses, have only unconsciously absorbed these details, to them the result of years of experience and practice. But the artist with properly trained eye and by visualizing the accepted type can pick out unerringly small variations, and by the faintest exaggeration of same depict the individual character (Plate V).

There is no necessity for the artist to be familiar with the separate bones of the horse's head. It is sufficient for him that they consist of upper and lower jaw, the most important point being the Zygomatic Ridge, no other animal having it developed in quite a similar manner

PLATE VI

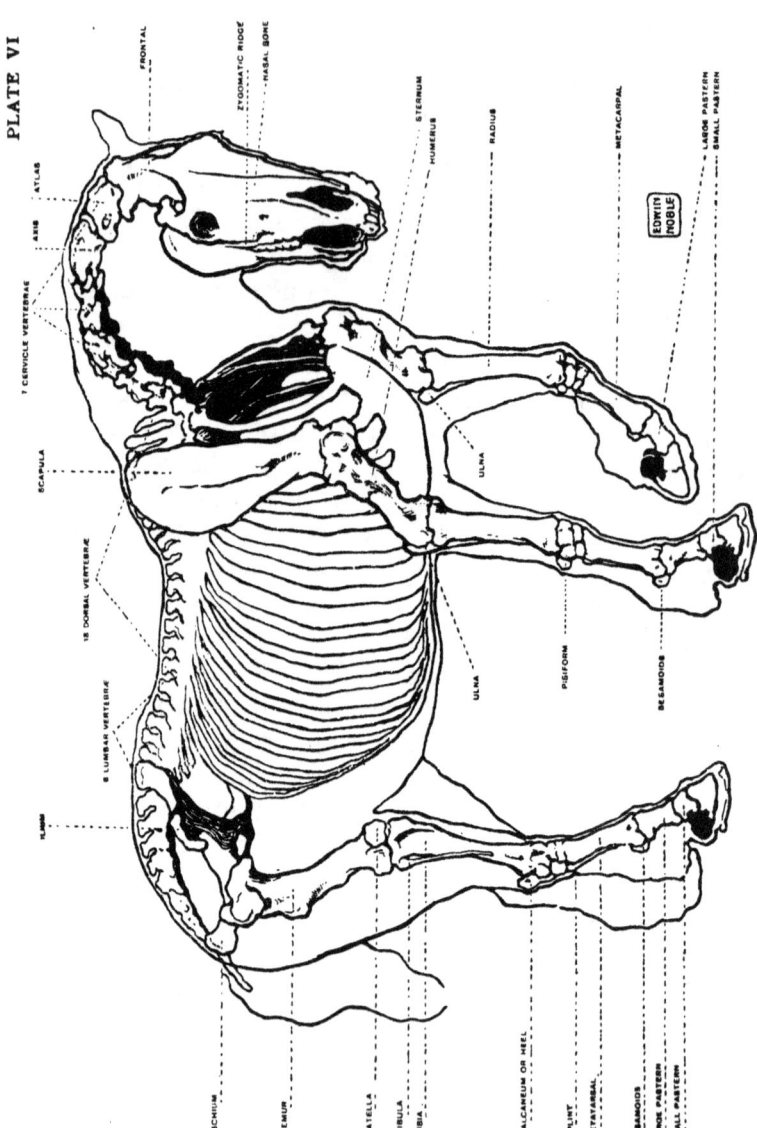

SKELETON OF A HORSE

FRONTAL
ZYGOMATIC RIDGE
NASAL BONE
ATLAS
AXIS
7 CERVICLE VERTEBRAE
STERNUM
HUMERUS
RADIUS
SCAPULA
METACARPAL
LARGE PASTERN
SMALL PASTERN
EDWIN NOBLE
ULNA
18 DORSAL VERTEBRAE
6 LUMBAR VERTEBRAE
ULNA
PISIFORM
SESAMOIDS
FLANK
ISCHIUM
FEMUR
PATELLA
FIBULA
TIBIA
CALCANEUM OR HEEL
SPLINT
METATARSAL
SESAMOIDS
LARGE PASTERN
SMALL PASTERN

In the proportions of the head, the lower point of the Zygomatic Ridge should about equally divide it in length, and the eye socket should again lay about midway between this and the top of the skull. These points are important as giving the position of the harness.

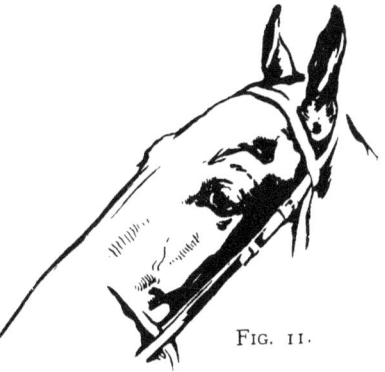

Fig. 11.

Note the shape and size of the ridge of bone above the eye socket (Fig. 11). Over this ridge rests the forehead strap, attaching to the cheek straps which lie behind the ears, and which follow the line of the Zygomatic Ridge down to the corner of the mouth. The nose band should lie exactly the width of two fingers below the point of Zygomatic Ridge.

The neck vertebræ (Plate VI) has little of interest to the artist owing to the heavy covering of powerful muscles. The *Atlas* bone is called after the mythological giant who supported the heavens upon his shoulders, the head being supported by this

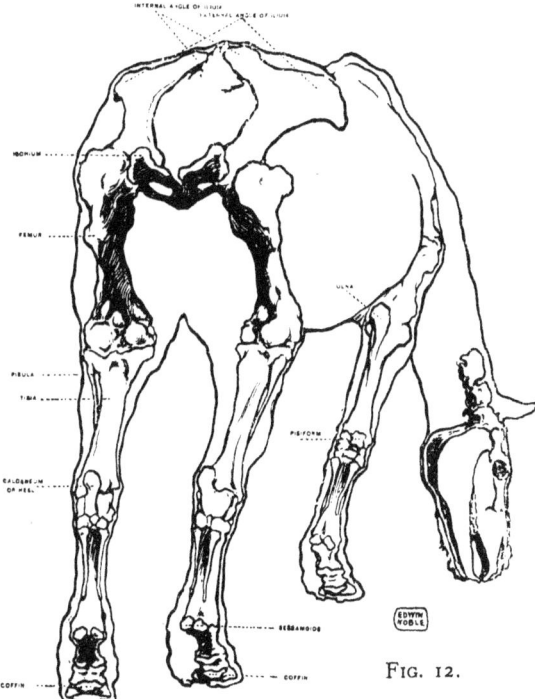

Fig. 12.

bone. The Axis is the next bone of the vertebral column, and, as its name denotes, is the axis upon which all movements are made.

The *Ribs* on either side number eighteen.

The bones of the forearm are *Scapula* or shoulder-blade.

The *Humerus*.

The *Radius* and *Ulna*, the latter two being fixed and inseparable. For this reason a horse cannot rotate the arm as in the Human or the Cat and Dog tribe. The action of the forearm of a Horse is merely to and fro, therefore it is unable to change direction suddenly when travelling at full speed, but must either take a wide sweep or reduce speed and pivot upon the hind legs.

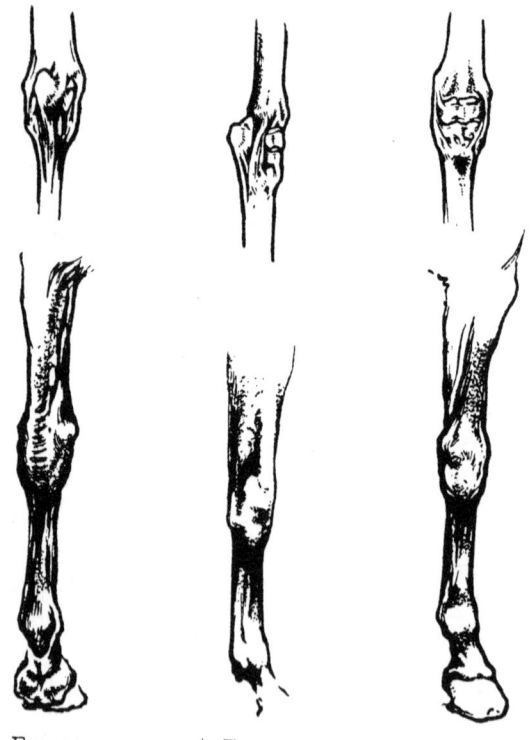

FIG. 13.   FIG. 14.   FIG. 15.

SHOWING THE JOINTS AND LIGAMENTS OF KNEE

The knee (Figs. 13 to 15), so called, of a horse is identical with the wrist of the human forearm. The collection of small bones are bound together, and enclosed by ligaments and covered by skin only ; it is, therefore, important to understand the general shape of the whole.

The *Metacarpus* consists of one large bone and two rudimentary ones, known as Splints. These, as previously pointed out, are the rudimentary second and fourth toes.

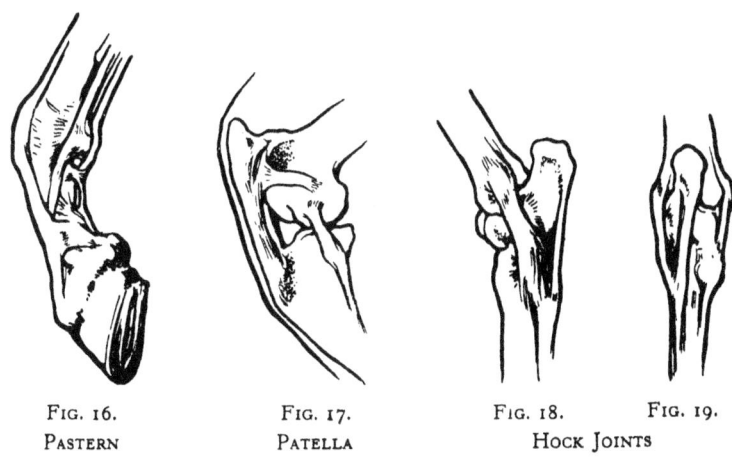

FIG. 16.   FIG. 17.   FIG. 18.   FIG. 19.
PASTERN   PATELLA   HOCK JOINTS

FETLOCK AND HOCK JOINTS

The Greater and Smaller Pasterns (Fig. 16) compare with the human finger joint with its bony covering of finger nail or *Hoof*.

The *Pelvis* (Fig. 12) has two very important projections, the *Ilium* and the *Ischium*, both of which have a tremendous influence upon the form, the *Pubis* bone being hidden.

The bones of lower limb are :—

The *Femur*.

The *Tibia* and the *Fibula*.

The *Patella* or Knee-cap (Fig. 17), as in the human knee, is merely attached to the Femur and Tibia by ligaments, but itself serves as a point of attachment for some important muscles, and in drawings of movement its position requires to be well understood, and in a similar manner, Figs. 18 to 19 show the ligaments which bind the hock or heel of the Horse.

The heel portions marked black in Plate vi are two fatty cushions which serve as buffers to lessen the effects of jarring or concussion upon the foot.

It will be noticed that no mention has been made of a *Clavicle* or Collar-bone. The purpose of this bone is to brace out the shoulders so as to give a free use to the arms. It is found in nearly all the birds, and in many of the climbing, burrowing, or flying animals, such as Squirrel, Mole, and Bat, but in the Horse and Dog it is quite absent, and in the Cat tribe is found in a very undeveloped state.

The important muscles of the head are :

The *Levator Nasolabialis* or *Maxillaris*, which is the elevator of upper lip and corner of mouth.

Zygomaticus, the action of which is to pull down the lower portion of the *Orbicularis*, or muscle of the eye, and to raise the corner of the mouth.

The *Nasalis*, which is attached to the cartilage of the nose and dilates the nostrils.

The *Caninus*, with similar action, also elevating the upper lip.

NOTE.—A Horse under the effects of excitement or violent action brings all the above muscles into movement. They, therefore, have an important influence upon light and shade and expression, and are made very visible by the cast shadow from nose band of bridle.

Muscles of lesser importance, inasmuch as they alter but little in shape, are the *Masseter*, giving the closing movement to the lower jaw ; the *Temporalis*, with similar action, and the *Buccinator*, which flattens the cheeks, thus pressing the food between the teeth and also retracting the corner of the mouth.

The neck is supported by a complicated and powerful series of deep-seated muscles, called the *Complexus*, but this is again covered by the *Splenius* muscle, originating in the mastoid process at the base of the skull and attaching to the transverse processes of the upper cervicle vertebræ. Its action is to extend or incline the head.

The *Longus Colli* is also a deep-seated muscle, originating from the first six dorsal vertebræ and attaching to underside of *Atlas*. Its action is to curve the whole neck downwards, and is partly covered by the *Splenius*.

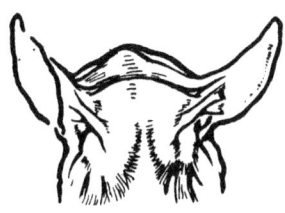

FIG. 20.

The *Serratus Magnus*, although not a superficial muscle, is of great importance, as its peculiar form is always well marked in well-bred and thin-skinned horses. It originates from the first seven ribs and the last five cervicle vertebræ by a series of digitations, and is inserted in the inner side of the *Scapula*. Its action is to attach and raise the trunk between the shoulder blades, and also to raise the ribs in inspiration, consequently may be plainly visible when the horse is breathing rapidly, such as after a race.

The *Caracohyoidaeus* is merely a flat membraneous tendon which covers the *Carotid Artery* and the main portion of the wind-pipe, or *Trachea*.

The *Sterno-Mastoideus* arises at the top of the *Sternum* and inserts into the lower jawbone under the *Parotid Gland*.

On the top of this lies the *Jugular Vein*.

Two small muscles shown in one plate only are the *Sterno-Thyroideus*, which arise from the Sternum and becoming tendinous partially cover the wind-pipe and insert into the *Thyroid* cartilages.

NOTE.—The Splenius passing over the *Atlas* and Axis bones becomes very fleshy and forms one single mass

PLATE VII

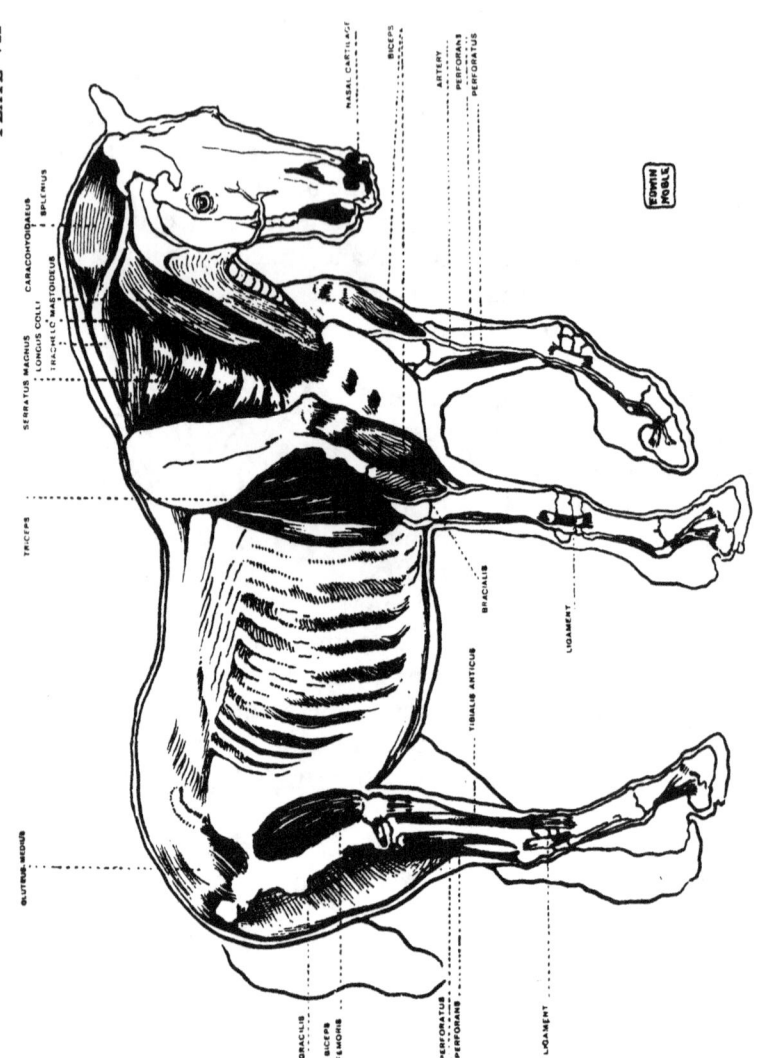

DEEP LAYER OF MUSCLES OF THE HORSE

very noticeable in all sideways movements, casting a heavy shadow upon the neck.

The Shoulder Muscles (Plate VII) are the *Triceps*, powerful muscles in three well-marked parts or heads. It originates from nearly the whole of the lower border of the

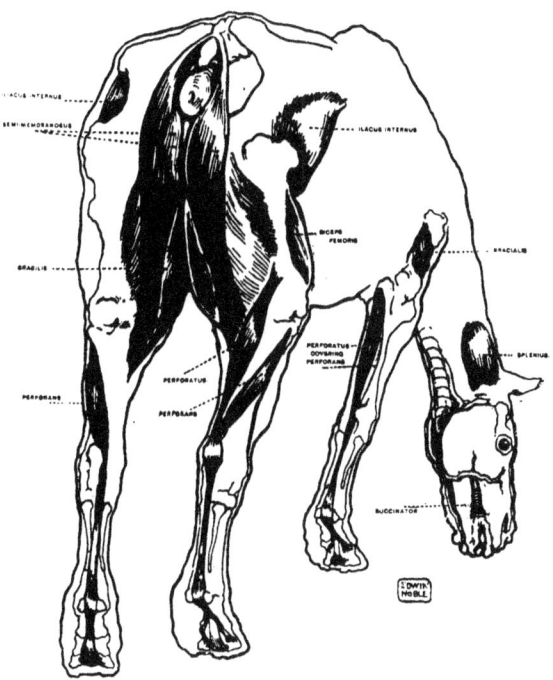

FIG. 21.

DEEP LAYER OF MUSCLES

Scapula, and also the inner and lower side of the *Humerus*, and inserts by tendons to the *Olecranon* or elbow. Its action is to extend the forearm.

A small muscle whose influence upon the surface can be plainly seen is *Teres Minor*. It originates from the lower edge of *Scapula*, and running across the biceps inserts in the *Humerus* near the top of the *Deltoid* ridge. It has an important action in the flexing of the shoulder joint.

PLATE VIII

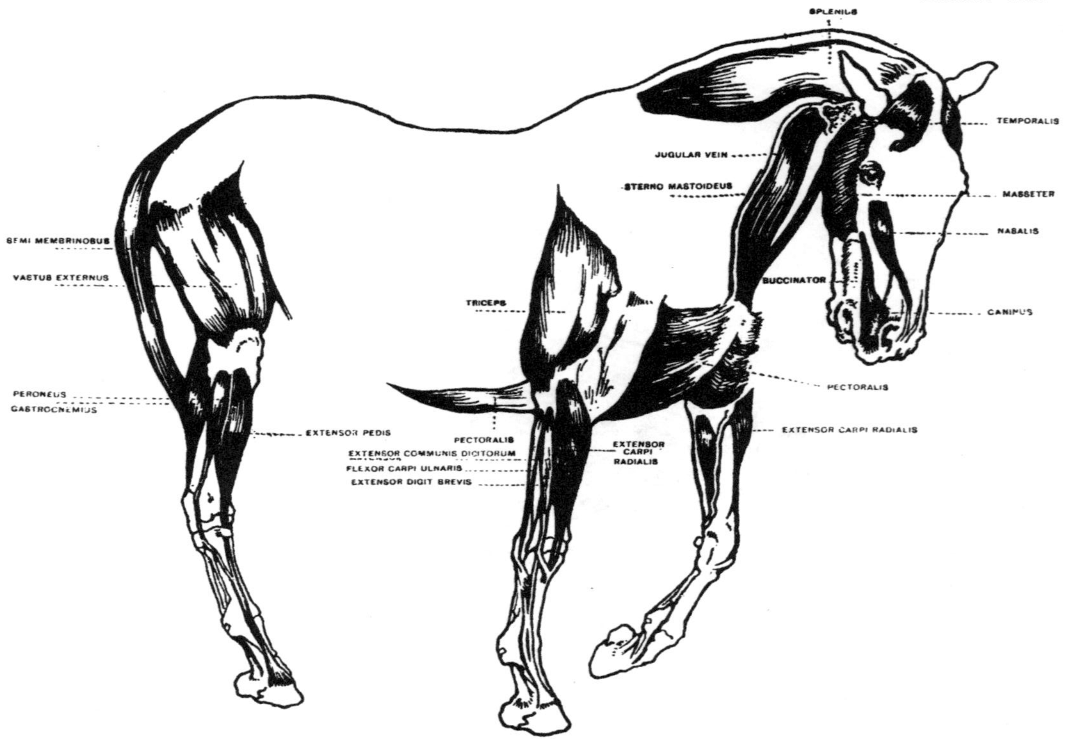

MUSCLES OF THE HORSE

TEMPORALIS

MASSETER

NASALIS

CANINUS

SPLENIUS

PECTORALIS

EXTENSOR CARPI RADIALIS

BUCCINATOR

JUGULAR VEIN

STERNO MASTOIDEUS

EXTENSOR CARPI RADIALIS

TRICEPS

PECTORALIS

EXTENSOR PEDIS

EXTENSOR COMMUNIS DIGTORUM

FLEXOR CARPI ULNARIS

EXTENSOR DIGIT BREVIS

SEMI MEMBRINOSUS

VASTUS EXTERNUS

PERONEUS

GASTROCNEMIUS

22

Infraspinatus, as its name denotes lies upon the lower side of the spine of *Scapula*, and *Supraspinatus* upon the whole surface above the spine of *Scapula*. It also extends the shoulder joint and assists in preventing dislocation.

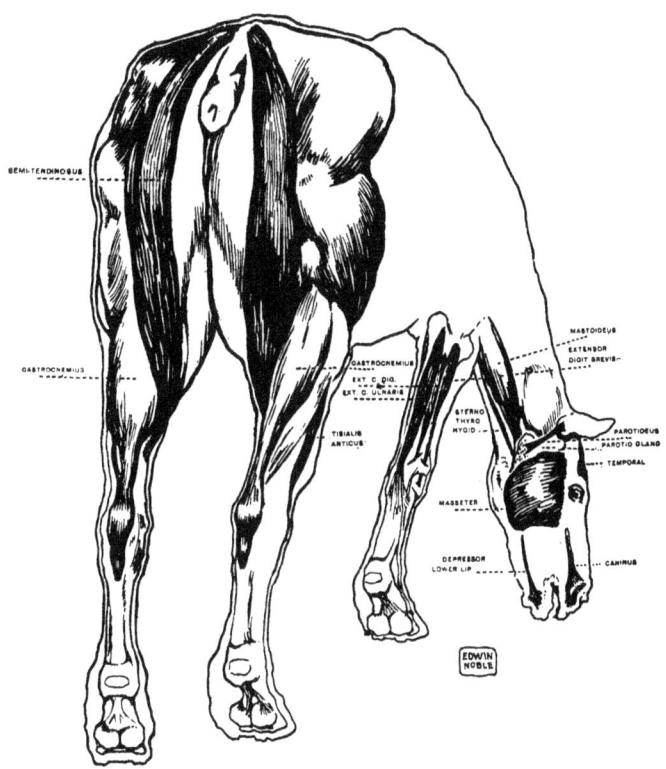

FIG. 22.
MUSCLES OF THE HORSE

The *Trapezius*.

The *Longissimus Dorsi* is the most important muscle in the trunk, and is again covered by the fascia-like *Latissimus Dorsi*.

The *Pectoralis* is an important muscle, inasmuch as it varies considerably in the different breeds of horses. Much

PLATE IX

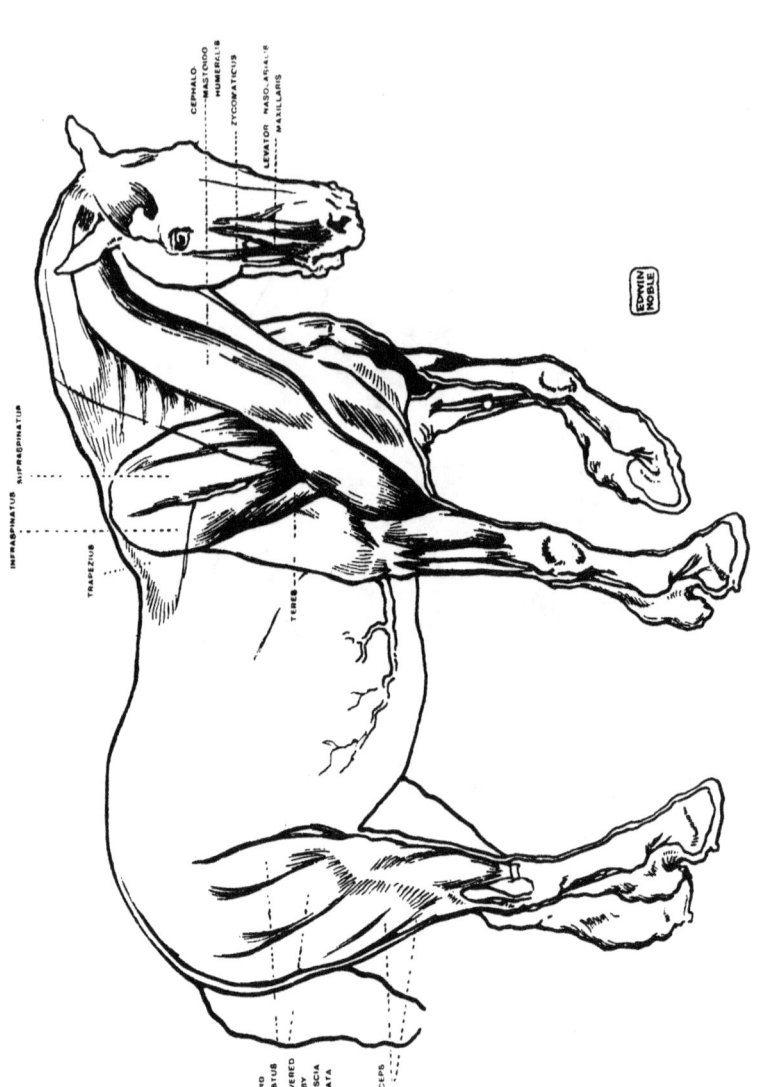

CEPHALO-
MASTOIDO
HUMERALIS
ZYGOMATICUS
LEVATOR NASO-LABIALIS
MAXILLARIS

INFRASPINATUS SUPRASPINATUS
TRAPEZIUS
TERES

LONG VASTUS COVERED BY FASCIA LATA
BICEPS

EDWIN NOBLE

SURFACE MUSCLES OF THE HORSE

of the pulling power depends upon this muscle, its action being to draw the shoulder and arm downwards and backwards. In a similar manner to the *Pectoralis* of the human figure, this muscle splits up into bundles, very marked in the chest of a man of great physical development, and the same tendency may be found in the chest of a powerful, heavy draught horse.

The three most important muscles in the movement of the front leg are the *Biceps* and the *Bracialis*, the action of both being to flex the forearm, whilst the *Triceps*, a prominent muscle with its clearly marked four divisions, extends the forearm.

There are six Extensors in the forearm, but only three require notice. *Extensor Carpi Radialis* is a powerful muscle arising from the outer side of

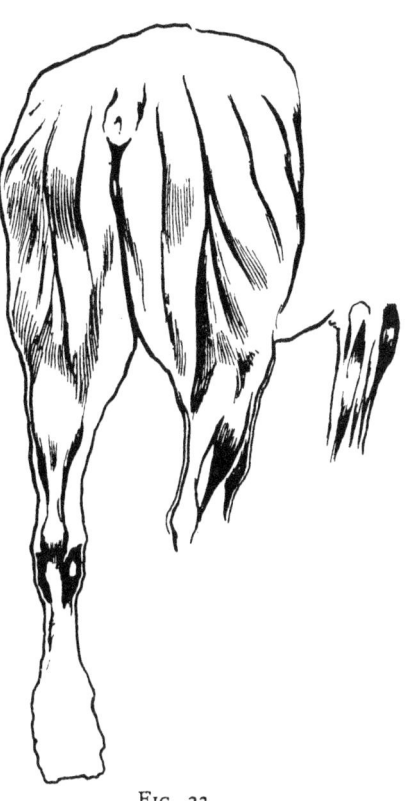

FIG. 23.
SURFACE MUSCLES

Humerus and becoming tendinous as it passes over the knee, inserts upon the upper end of the *Metacarpal*; its action is to extend the forearm.

Extensor Digitorum Communis and *Extensor Digitorum Brevis* passing over the knee downwards to finally unite and insert upon the lower pastern. Their action is to extend the foot.

There are seven Flexors.

The *Perforans* or *Deep Flexor* arises on the inner *Epicondyle* of the *Humerus*, and becoming tendinous, passes on the inner side of *Pisiform* bone, and over the *Sesamoids*, finally dividing and inserting into the *Coffin Bone* or *Navicular*.

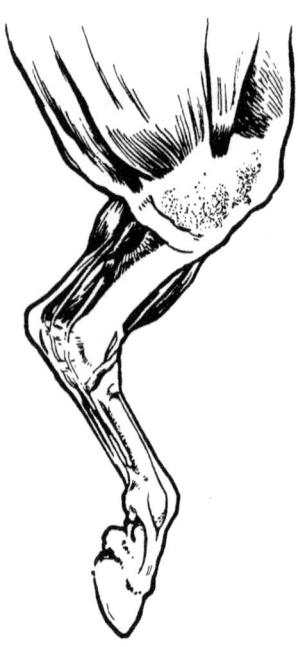

FIG. 24.
INSIDE OF THE THIGH MUSCLE

NOTE.—This latter bone is small and embedded in the hoof. (See back view.)

The *Perforatus* or superficial *Flexor* arises from immediately above the previous muscle, and follows the same course until it passes over the *Sesamoids*, when it divides and inserts into the lower edge of either side of the lower pastern.

Flexor Carpi Ulnaris (Plate IX) is a very obvious muscle, which inserts into the *Pisiform*. The action of all these, as the name denotes, is to flex the arm and foot.

NOTE.—Both *Perforans* and *Perforatus*, although deep-seated muscles, have important bearing upon the drawing of a horse's leg, if the fact of their becoming tendinous is properly realised.

After passing behind *Pisiform*, and held in their place by a ligamentous wrapping, they stretch down the leg and over the *Sesamoids* in a perfectly straight line. Any curving of this line at once depicts weakness and lameness.

The muscles of the hind limb are the *Gluteus*, which practically covers the upper part of the *Pelvis*.

The *Gracilis* (Fig. 21), which arises from the *Pubic* region and inserts into the inner side of the *Tibia*; its action is to adduct the thigh.

The *Biceps Femoris*, which flexes the leg.

The *Semitendinosus* (Fig. 22), which originates on the *Ischiatic* tuberosity and passes by a tendon into the *Tibia* and the *Semimembranosus*, which arises from almost the same spot with similar insertion, but showing as two separate muscles in their fleshy passage.

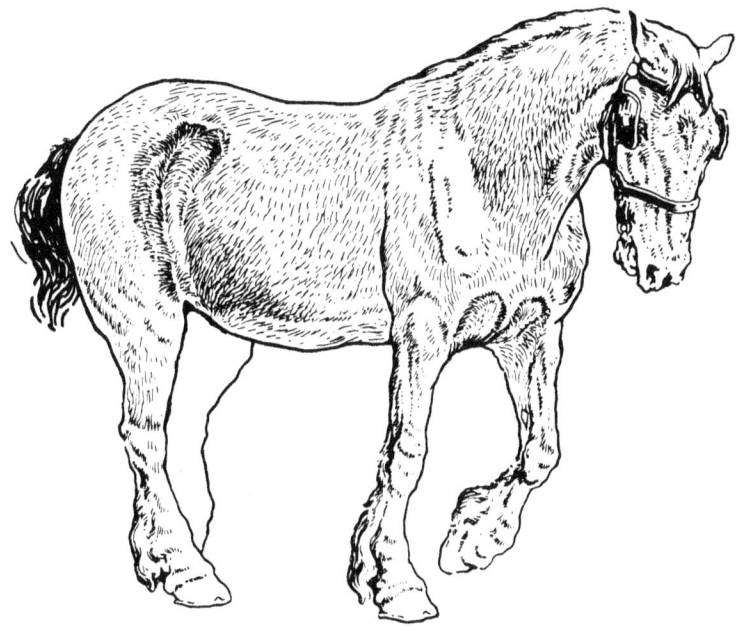

FIG. 25.
SHOWING THE DIRECTION OF THE HAIR TRACTS

Fig. 23 shows the general surface appearance of the muscles.

Their action is to adduct the thigh and flex the stifle joint. The *Sartorius* is a muscle upon the inside of the thigh and is visible in jumping or rearing positions (Fig. 24).

Examination of Plate v will suggest a more complicated muscular development than is shown by the diagrams in certain portions of the body, notably the chest.

PLATE X

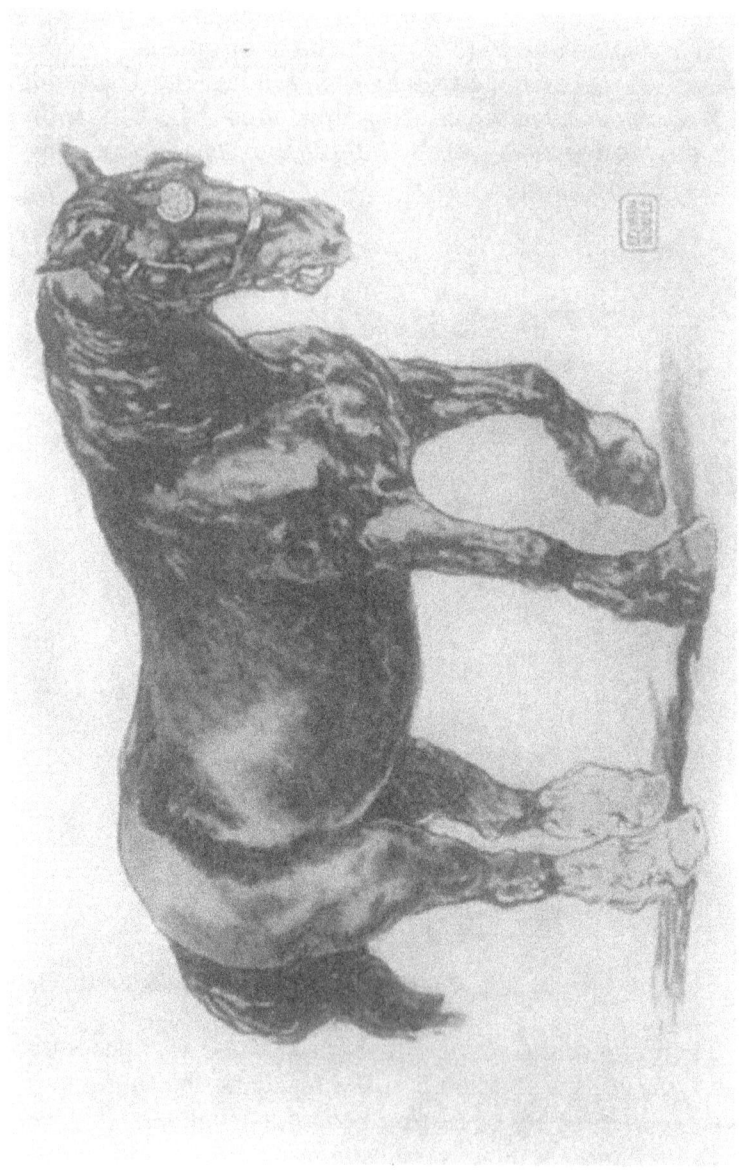

STUDY OF A HORSE

SHOWING THE PLAY OF LIGHT AND SHADE UPON THE SHEEN OF THE COAT

This appearance, however, is caused by the play of light falling upon the hair which at some points entirely changes direction.

Fig. 25 shows the direction of the hair tracts, and attention should be directed upon the manner in which it passes forward between the forelegs and meeting the downward directed hairs upon the *Pectoral* muscles of the chest causes a distinct radiation, with the direct consequence that the light will fall upon the hair in one spot in such a manner as to give the sheen, and in another to give the local colour of the hair only. The same alteration of direction will be found upon the flanks of the horse.

PLATE XI

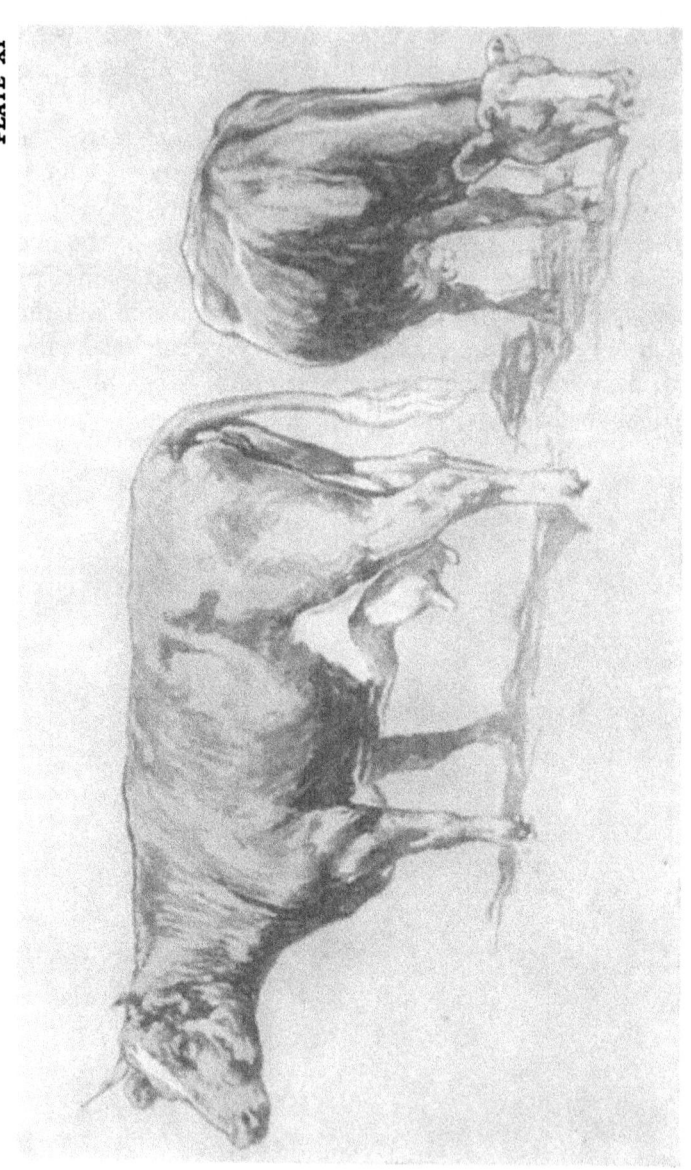

STUDY OF COWS

CHAPTER III

THE COW

A BRIEF statement of the differences in structure of the horse and the cow is all that is necessary, and it will be found that these are more apparent than real. Comparison of the two skeletons (Plate XII) will quickly show the principal points of variation, the *Cervicle Vertebræ* being shorter and the *Spinous Processes* of the *Dorsal Vertebræ* being longer, with a corresponding increase in the height of the *Scapula*, with the result that the neck appears thicker and to be set lower on the shoulders than it does in the horse.

The ribs are thirteen in number on either side.

The skull of the cow is more clearly pyramidal and is shorter and wider. The feet, however, are the points where the greatest variation occurs, Four *Digits* being present, whilst the *Splint* bones are absent. The two *Digits* which form the cleft hoof have three *Phalanges* and three *Sesamoids* each. The second and fifth, which are mere *Vestigas*, and are placed behind the fetlock, do not articulate with the bones of the leg.

The very marked difference in the external appearance of the cow is due, however, to the considerable alteration which takes place in the bulk and shape of some of the muscles. Certain of these brought into action by the horse in the motions of jumping or galloping are totally undeveloped in the cow, whilst, on the contrary, the production of flesh for food purposes has caused the development of totally different features in this animal.

PLATE XII

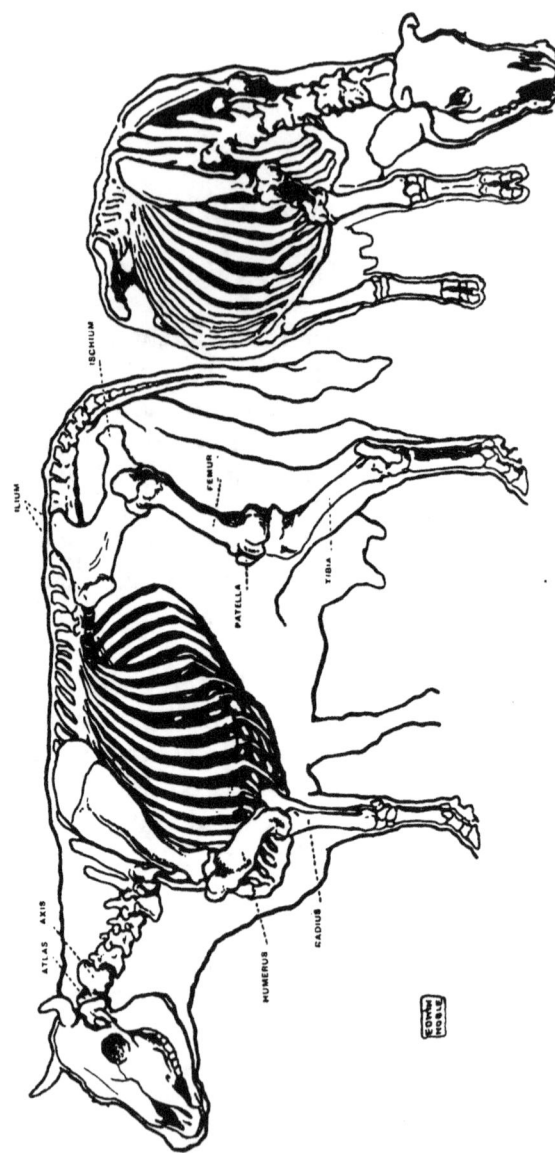

SKELETON OF A COW

PLATE XIII

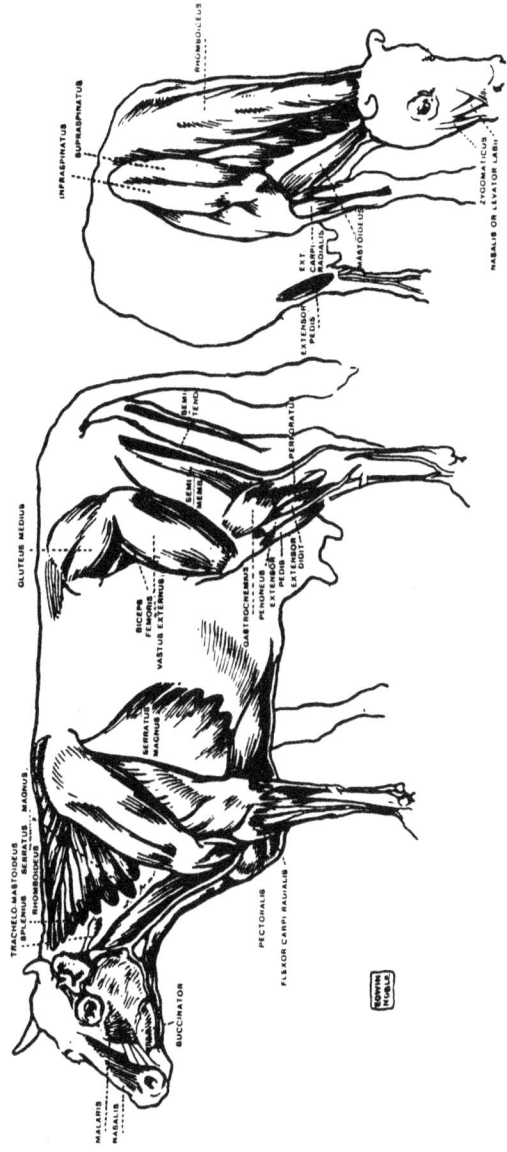

MUSCLES OF A COW

33

On the face, the *Frontalis* muscle, which is relatively unimportant in the horse, is greatly developed and practically covers the greater part of the *Nasalis* muscle. The *Zygomaticus* is again more developed, whilst the *Malaris* spreads over the cheek in a broad mass.

NOTE.—The muzzle of the cow has very little movement when compared with the mobile lips of the horse, and hence the lesser development of the muscles governing same.

In the neck the *Splenius* presents different features. It is quite a thin muscle and partly blends with several others, principally the *Trachelo Mastoideus*, which is, again, a small muscle in comparison with that of the horse. The *Rhomboideus* is well developed, however, and extends further and is covered by the *Trapezius*, again much thicker and broader. In the forearm there is little difference, with the exception of the tendons, which in most cases divide, a branch extending to each digit.

The Biceps *Femoris* and *Vastus Externus* are larger, also the *Fascia Lata*, which extends lower (Plate XIII).

The *Semitendinosus* and the *Semimembranosus* arise on the *Ischium* only, and are quite small and unimportant. Their absence explains the principal cause of the difference in the appearance of the hind-quarters of these two animals.

It should be realised that the entire system of the cow is devoted to the production of milk, and that the formation of flesh interferes with this function, hence the prominence of such points as the *Ilium* and *Ischium*, *Scapula*, *Ribs*, etc., etc. In bullocks, these points are not so prominent owing to the greater amount of flesh carried, the ideal animal from the butchers' and breeders' point of view being that with a back as straight and as broad as a billiard table.

There does not appear to be any laws governing the colour patches of cattle in a wild state, all being whole coloured ; neither does the hair take any distinct changes of

PLATE XIV

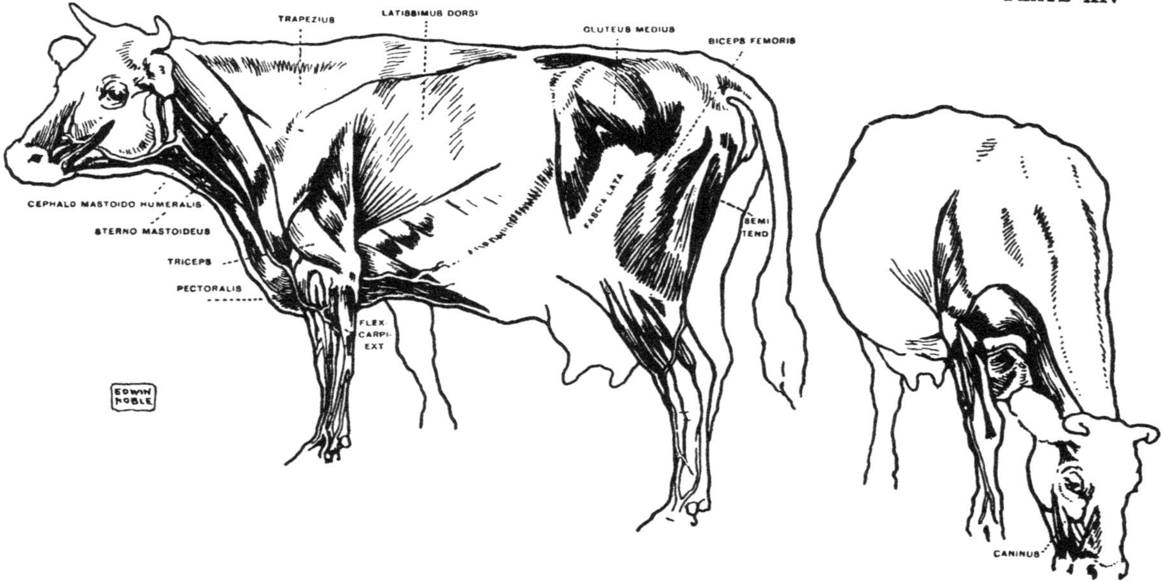

CANINUS

GEMI TEND

BICEPS FEMORIS

GLUTEUS MEDIUS

FASCIA LATA

LATISSIMUS DORSI

TRAPEZIUS

FLEX CARPI EXT

CEPHALO MASTOIDO HUMERALIS

STERNO MASTOIDEUS

TRICEPS

PECTORALIS

EDWIN NOBLE

SURFACE MUSCLES OF A COW

direction, sufficient, that is, to affect the artist, the only obvious point being the star upon the forehead.

For characterisation purposes, special attention should be paid to the heavy wrinkling of the loose skin upon jaw, at the elbows, and upon the neck, especially with any sideways movements; similar actions in the horse showing but little wrinkling

CHAPTER IV

THE DOG

M ANY efforts have been made to trace the ancestry of the modern domestic dog, and although some scientists are inclined to dispute the fact, on the grounds of insufficient evidence, it is now almost universally recognised that to the wolf tribe must we look for the original parents. Whatever may be the doubts of a Zoological scientist, there are none so far as the artist is concerned. To the wolf alone does he look for his general type of dog, and however much the proportions of our different breeds may vary, the coat, with few exceptions, follows one rule, and conforms to certain clearly defined masses of hair growth. These masses may be found exaggerated or the reverse, but nevertheless all can be discerned as being variations of the growth of hair on the body of the wolf.

The hair of the wolf is of two kinds (Plate xvi), an outer covering of long, coarse, dark hairs acting as a thatch and growing through the fine wool next the skin. The importance of offering the smallest possible resistance to the passage of the animal through grass, bushes, or other obstacles, and the necessity for running off the rain, especially when lying down at rest, are the two important factors when considering the direction of hair, and this is complied with by the backward and downward direction taken throughout. There are, however, certain local requirements which necessitate a compromise ; for example, the radiation of the hair about the eye. The eye is protected from any small obstacle or flying object, such as flies, dust, etc., etc., which may have a tendency to be brushed into it, by the radiating

PLATE XV

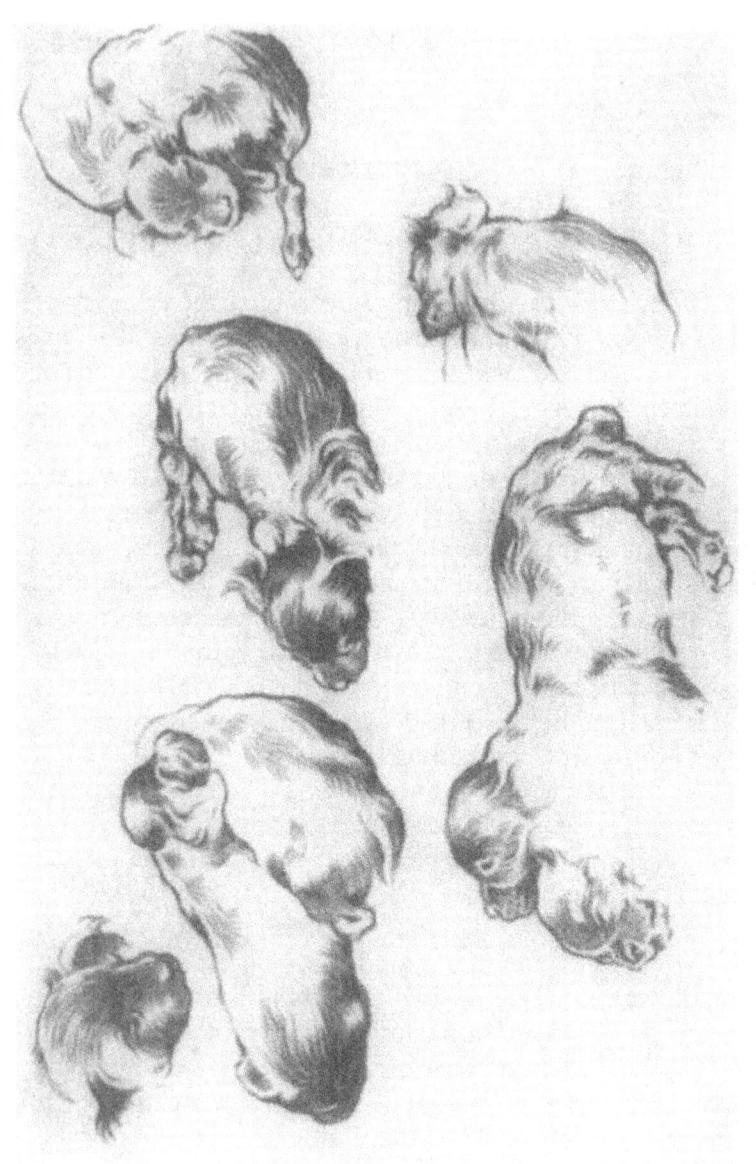

hair which, by coming into opposition with the upward
growing hair of the nose forms a little ridge which is so
marked a feature in the faces of most hairy animals.   Drops
of water, tears, etc., are also run off quickly, which would
not be the case if against the grain.   The radiation upon the
chest is accounted for by the hair upon ribs coming forward
and meeting the downward hair from throat and neck.
The necessity for preventing small objects from working

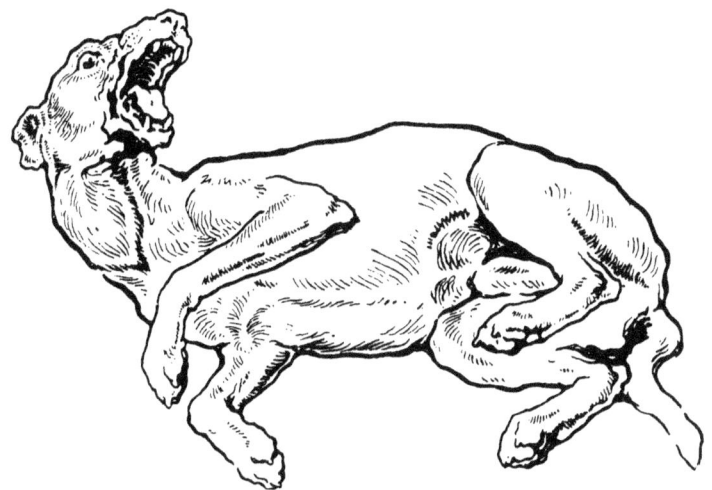

FIG. 26. SHOWING ARRANGEMENT OF HAIR

underneath the body, to become ticklish or troublesome to
the more vital organs, is possibly a reason again for this.

The drawing of a dog lying upon its side (Plate XVII)
shows how important is the knowledge of the hair growth.
In a slight sketch such as this, the art of suggestion is all
important, and every touch, however tentative, should be
full of meaning; therefore the greater the necessity to
differentiate clearly the lines which denote shadow, structural form or hair.   For the same reason the drawings of
puppies are introduced, the curves of infancy and the
colour being suggested by the hair alone.

PLATE XVI

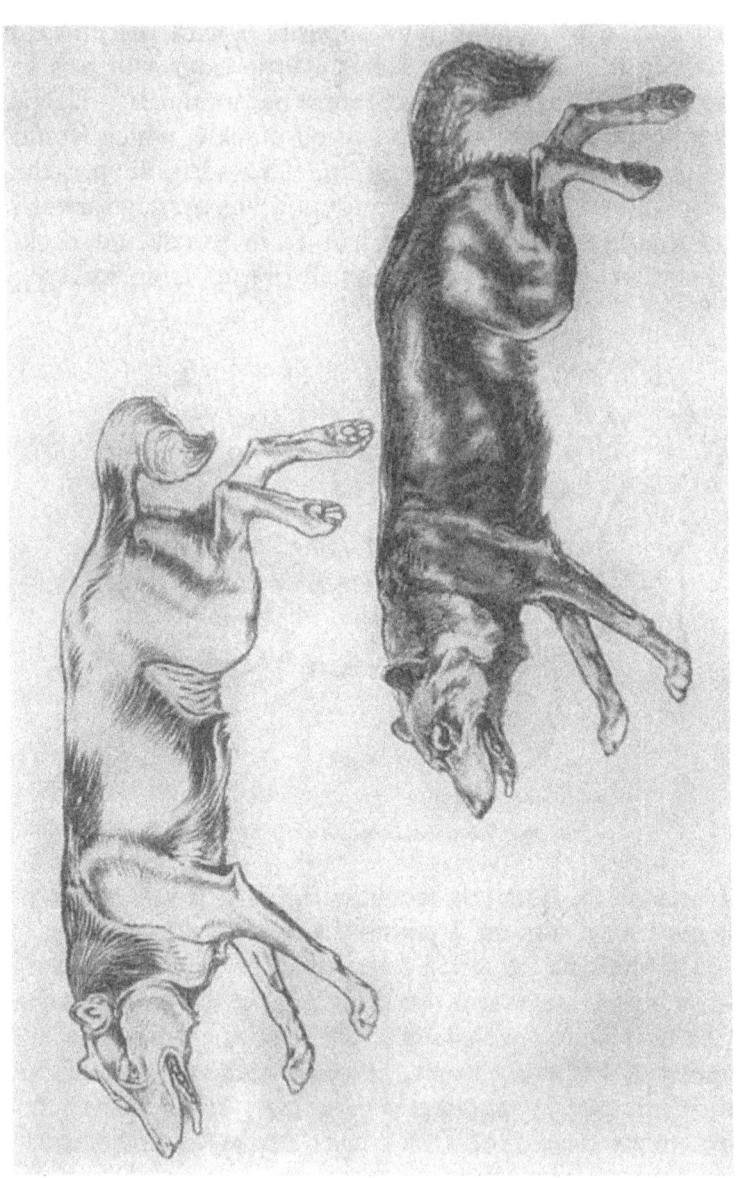

STUDY OF A WOLF
WITH DIAGRAM SHOWING THE ARRANGEMENT OF THE COAT

In examining the drawing of the wolf, note the furtive, cruel expression so characteristic of the animal. The following points contribute to that impression: The movement of the upper lip, showing the tremendous length of jaw; the oblique angle at which eyes are set in the skull; the stealthy action as shown by length of stride covering ground with least possible exertion or noise; the carriage of the tail, growing well below the level of the back, and seldom raised unless in action, as shown in drawing. When standing or walking the tail is always carried well down between the hind-legs, a mark of cowardice when seen in a dog. It is interesting to mark the carriage of tail through the various breeds of dogs (Fig. 27); the greater the distance between them and their ancestor, the wolf, the higher and more erect the tail is carried, finally reaching the extreme limit in the artificial toy dog, such as the Pom. and the Pekingese spaniel, where it is carried so high as to fall over the back in the form of a plume.

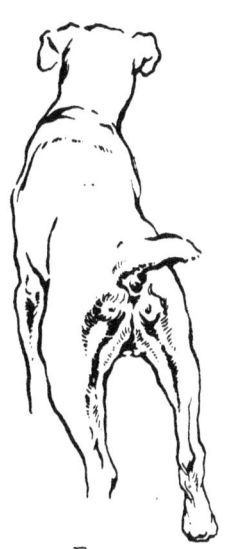

FIG. 27.
BACK VIEW OF TERRIER

Exceptions to this, however, are found in the Chow and the Esquimaux or Samoyede, both being decidedly wolf-like in character and ways, and the latter are, in fact, often interbred directly with the wolf.

The coat of a Collie (Plate XVIII and Fig. 28) follows very closely the arrangement of that of the wolf. The cheek patches, however, are lengthened, and fall downwards instead of standing out from the sides, and by merging into the long ruffle of neck hair, become the magnificent front and collar of the Collie. The masses of hair upon the back are clearly shown, and the exaggeration of the hair upon

PLATE XVII

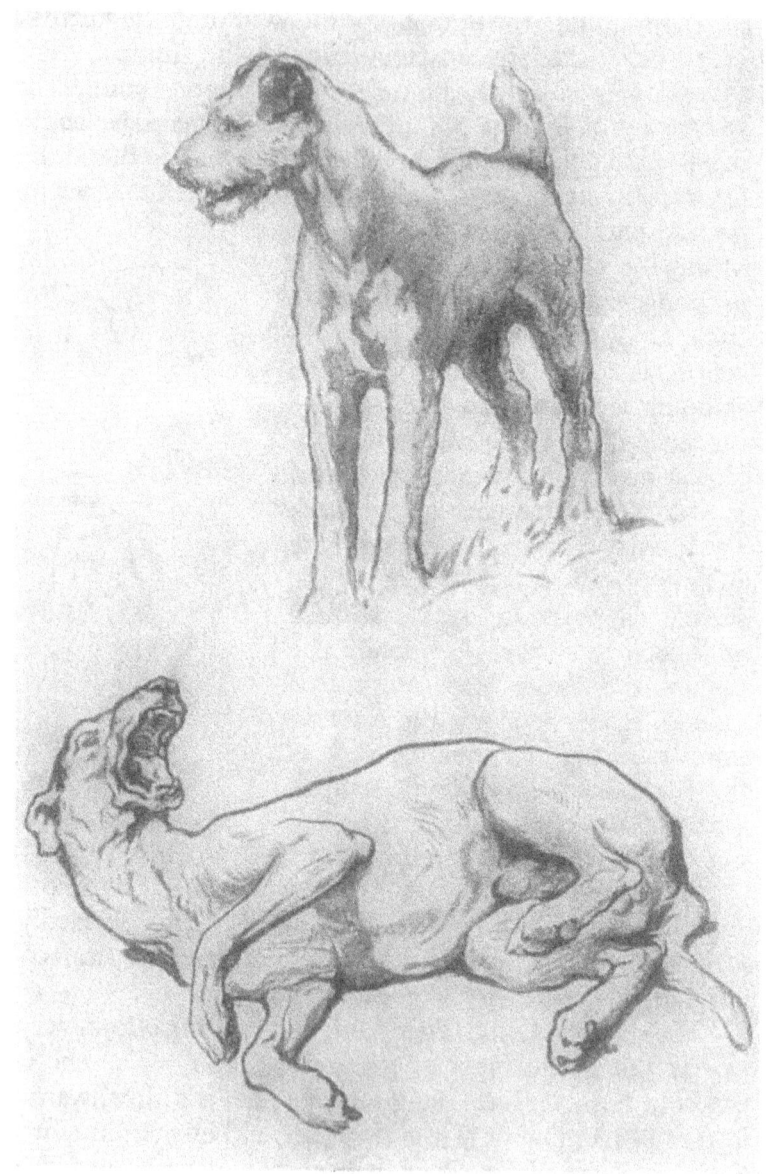

WIRE-HAIRED TERRIER
SNARLING DOG

back of forelegs forms the feathering. Note how the colour follows these changes of hair.

The expression of the head becomes less wolfish, the eyes being rounder and set more at right angles to the centre line of skull. The ears, whilst remaining erect, droop at the extreme tips. The legs, whilst appearing shorter, are not actually so, being due to the increased heaviness of the body and the long hair. The tail is set slightly higher at the root and is carried in a gayer fashion.

NOTE.—The degree of breeding of a Collie can usually be told at a glance by this point. A mongrel Collie will

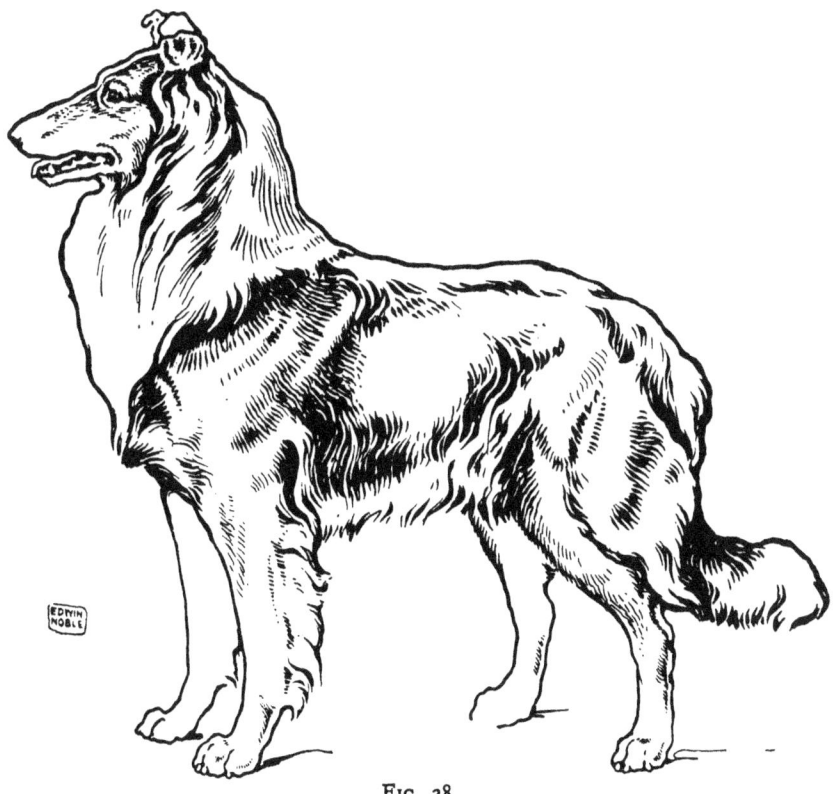

FIG. 28.
THE COAT OF A COLLIE

PLATE XVIII

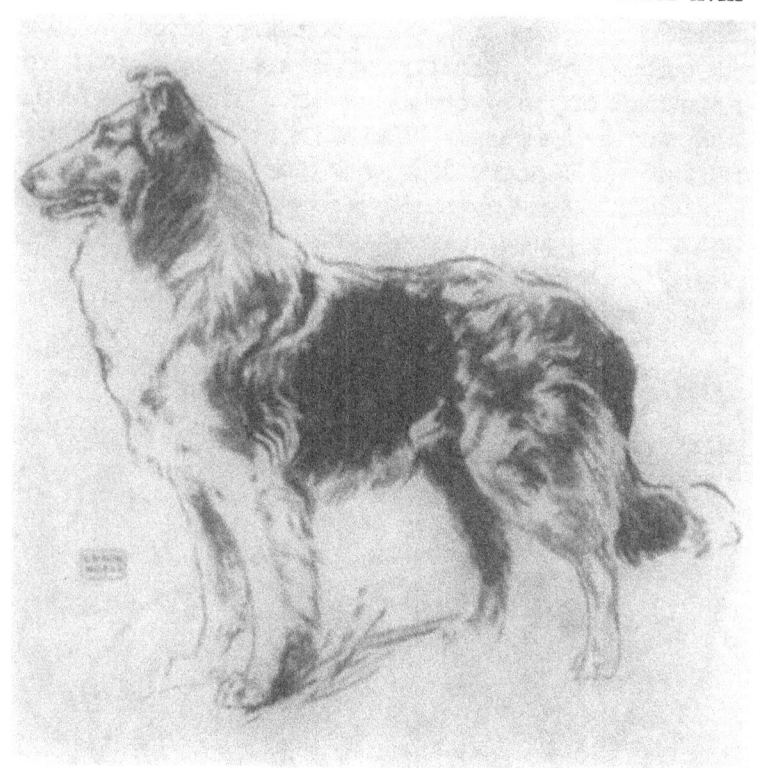

A COLLIE

carry his tail in wolf fashion without a curl, whilst a well-bred dog always curls the tip upwards. The feet, as in all the dogs built for speed, are small and compact.

The Collie gets his name from the word "Colly," which is the old-fashioned title of the Highland black-faced sheep, and as he is undoubtedly a dog of the Highlands, the Collie dog means a "Sheep dog."

In comparing the coat of a Chow (Plate xix) the cheek patches are again prominent, but not so as to fall in a downward direction. They stand erect from the face and form a complete surrounding collar or ruffle, which is again repeated by the neck fur, thus forming a double collar. The hair is rough and wiry in texture, appearing as if "on end," and does not lie close to the body anywhere. The ears are still of the wolf type, but a greater expression of intelligence is given to the face by the rounder eyes and heavy thoughtful brow. The hair upon the thighs is similar to the wolf and the Collie, but the tail is carried erect, falling over the back,

NOTE.—The Esquimaux and Samoyede are similar in coat arrangement and all three breeds show a short-legged sturdy type, built more for strength than speed.

The beautiful silken texture of the Spaniel's coat (Plate xx) is in direct contrast to all the previous dogs ; it is flat and wavy, forming small curls upon the ears, which are long and pendulous. They start low down upon the side of the skull, thus giving full prominence to its broad domed shape. There are no vestiges of any cheek patches or ruffle, but the chest is well covered with curls. The thigh patches again do not grow as on the Collie, but in the form of curls extending down to the hocks. The feet are broad and open. All the Spaniel breeds are as much at home in water as on dry land, being bred for the express purpose of flushing birds whose habitat are swampy lands and edges of rivers, lakes, etc. Therefore, the wide open foot supports their weight upon the spongy ground, at the same time giving a broad paddle for swimming. Between the toes

PLATE **XIX**

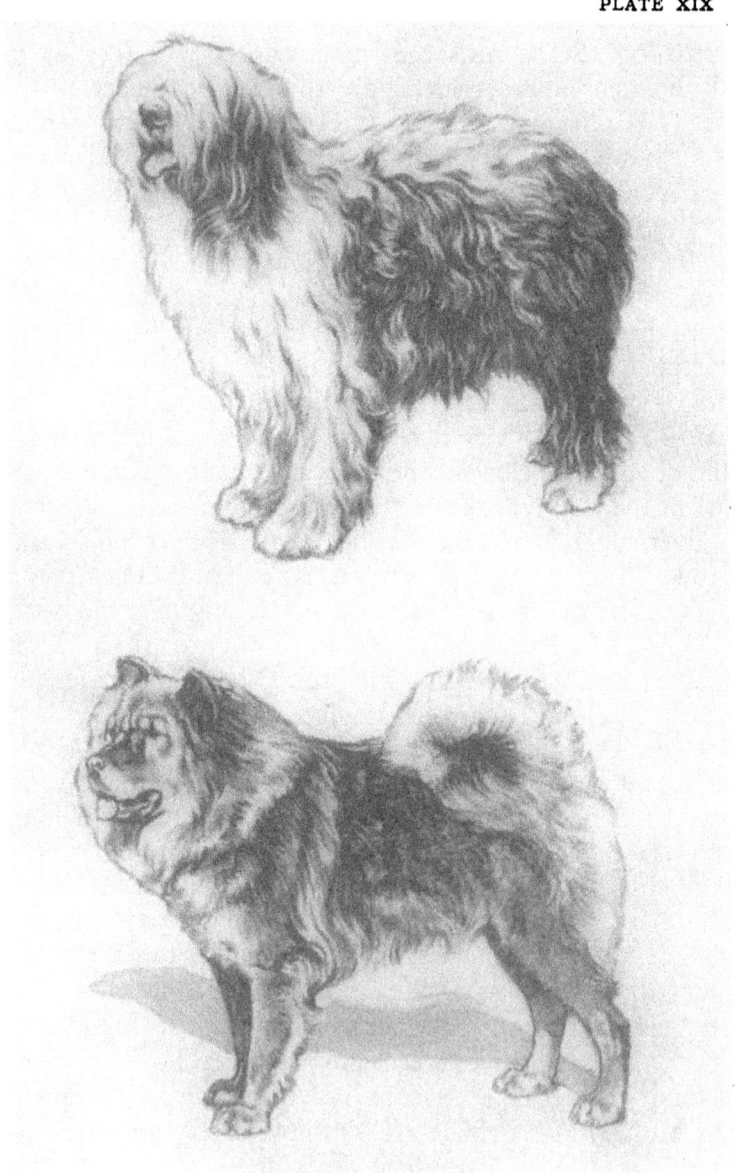

BOBTAIL SHEEP DOG

CHOW

46

is usually found a thick growth of coarse hair, which serves as a protection against injury to the tender portions between.

The Scottish Terrier (Plate XXI) possesses little beauty from the point of view of the painter, being square and stocky, with a large, ugly head and a harsh coat. His companionable qualities, however, atone for this deficiency, and as a sportsman he is hard to beat.

The hair masses are hardly distinguishable, owing to the even growth of coat, and it is interesting to note that there is not any change of colour, due to the same fact.

In this breed the head takes a different character entirely owing to the hair. A fierceness of aspect is given by the suggestion of beard and moustache, whilst the eyes are partially obscured by the longer hair of the nose being forced upwards and outwards by the radiation of that about the eyes. The cheek tufts are absent, also the neck ruffle, although a suggestion of their presence can be detected by the manner in which the hair curls at these points. The converging masses of the throat can be seen forming a ridge on either side down to the chest, where it again meets the hair, arising from between the forelegs.

NOTE.—The different form taken here when compared with the skin of a horse. The longer hair upon the back is not conspicuous, but can be faintly traced, and upon the fore limbs it forms a distinct ridge at elbow, and from thence down to the wrist. Upon the hind limbs it extends as far as the hock.

Both the Poodle (Plate XXII) and the Sheep dog (Plate XIX) are the exceptions to the general rule as to hair arrangement. In these two dogs the hair has been artificially developed to such an extent that it completely hides the form of the body beneath, and the equal density of growth showing but little change in direction has given them something of the lack of character seen in the sheep. In cases such as this, it is upon shadow masses only that the artist is forced to rely.

PLATE XX

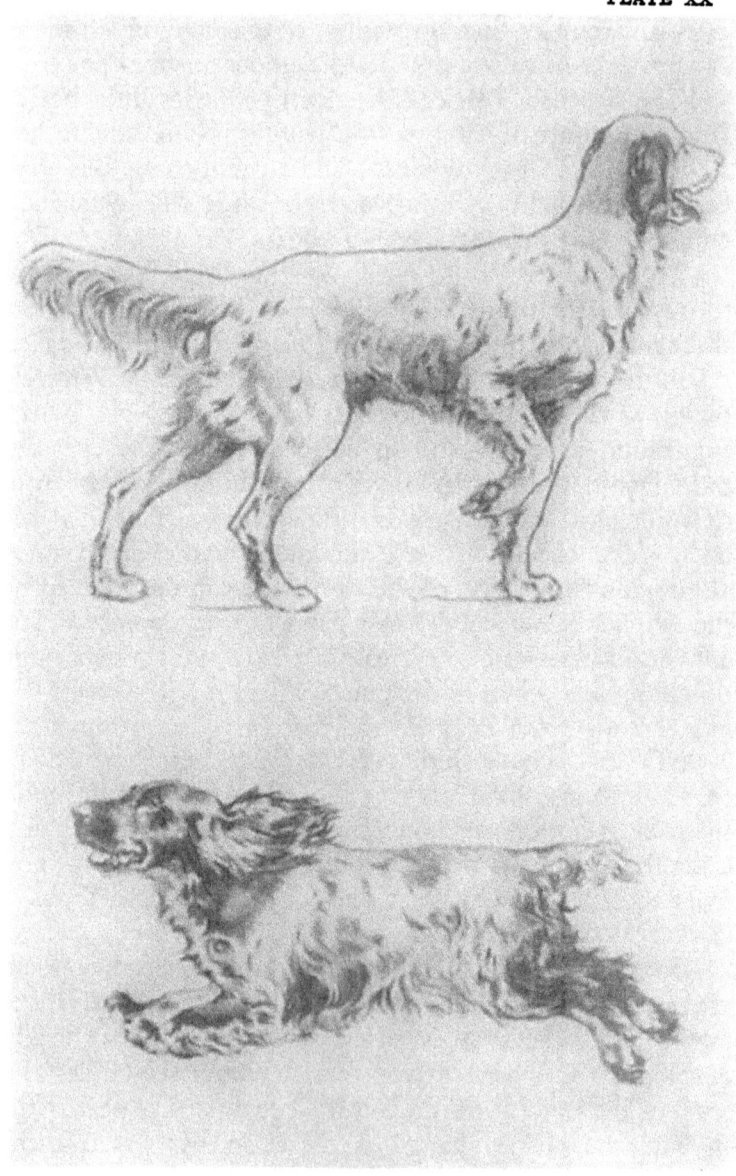

SETTER
SPANIEL

48

PLATE XXI

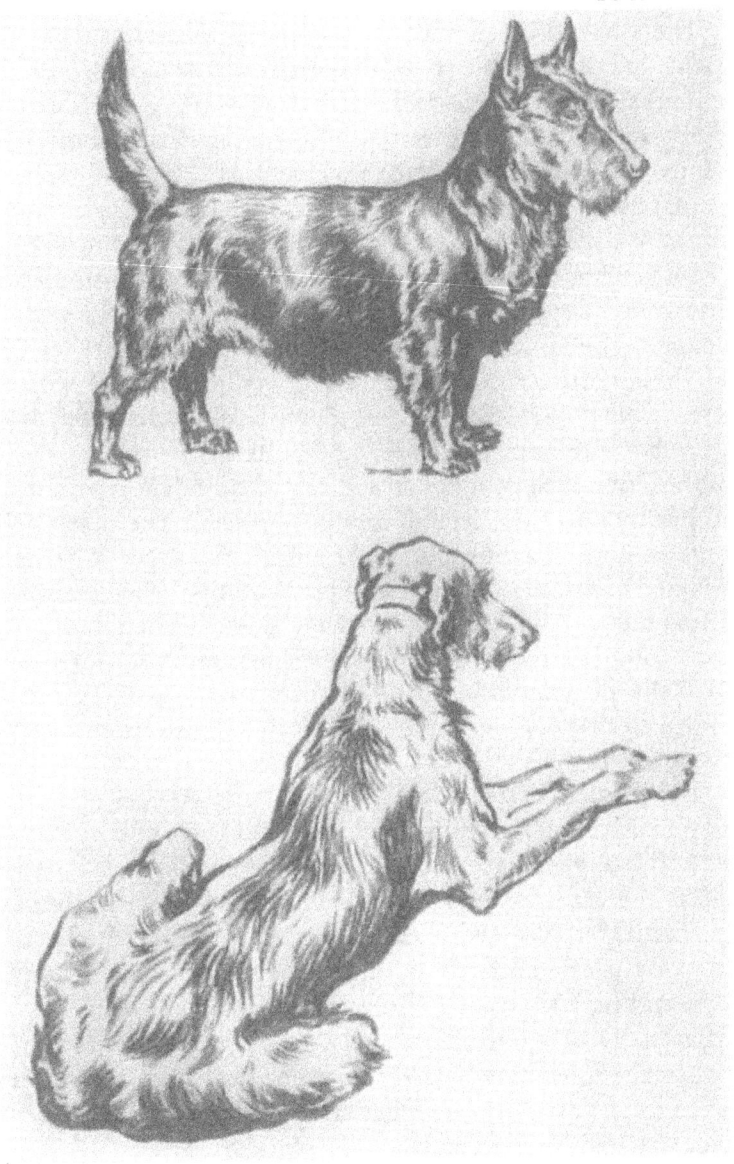

SCOTTISH TERRIER

DEERHOUND

The Sheepdog should be a powerful, tireless beast, capable of considerable speed under all circumstances. His well-developed and powerful hind-quarters give him a rolling action when trotting, similar to that of a bear, a likeness accentuated by the movement of the coat. The peculiarity of this breed being tailless is supposed to date from the time of the Conquest, when dogs for hunting purposes were the exclusive possessions of the great nobles. A powerful dog, however, was very necessary to the serfs to protect the flocks and herds from attacks of wolves, etc., and these were marked by "tawing" or cutting off three toes. This so interfered with their running that the tail was substituted for the toes, and it is possible that the Sussex Bobtail Sheepdog is a direct descendant of these, and has by selection become a tailless breed. The mark or badge denoting a Sheepdog has until quite recent years remained as a tailless dog, such being exempt from licence duties, and, in the opinion of many ancient shepherds, a tailless dog is preferable with sheep, because without this ornament he cannot turn so quickly, and is, therefore, obliged to make wider circles, thus causing less excitement and flurry to the sheep.

The English Setter (Plate xx) is a dog greatly beloved by all animal painters, owing to its beautiful form and colour. The soft, silky coat is more like the plumage of a bird, and reflects the varying sky and surroundings, whilst the clinging texture shows every play of muscle and movement. Only on the ears and throat, tail and legs can be found any curls, and here they are full of dainty and subtle lines.

In the Deerhound (Plate xxi) we have another graceful dog, but requiring an entirely different treatment to do full justice to its beauties. The general ruggedness of character is accentuated by the brows.

That the Greyhound (Plate xxiii) is of very ancient descent there is not the slightest doubt. The dogs depicted upon many Greek and Egyptian vases and Assyrian sculp-

PLATE XXII

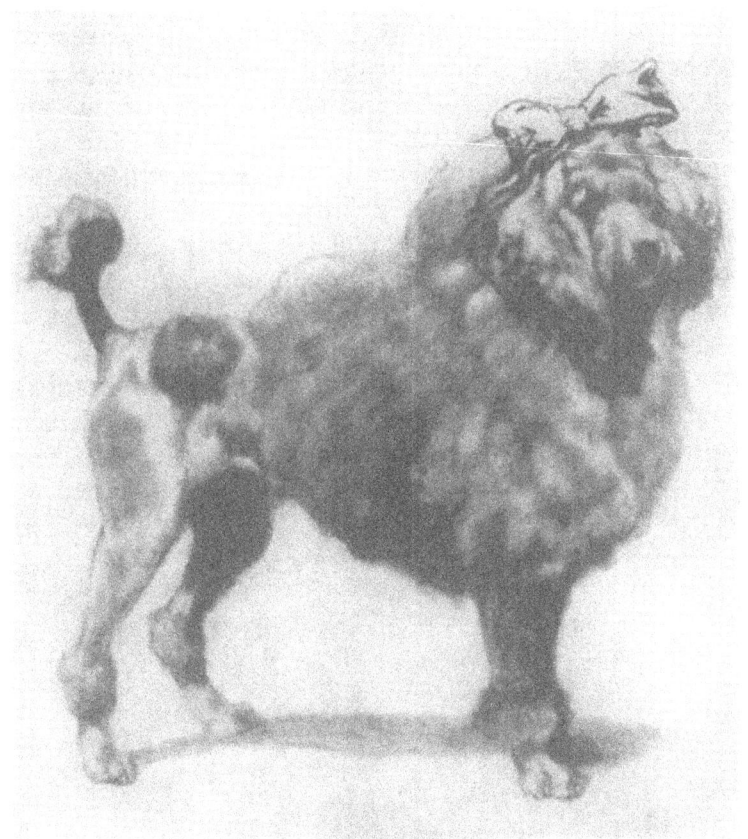

POODLE

tures show a thin, long-legged dog, not unlike our modern Greyhound, and many authorities are inclined to think that this breed is really one of the purest forms left of the olden time dog, and owing to its having been always used for the same purpose, namely, the swift pursuit of and capture of some smaller fleeing animal, there has been little inducement to alter his shape, or, in other words, we may presume any alterations were not a success.   Certainly, it is more than a coincidence that three animals built for speed, namely, the Hunter, the Greyhound and the Deer, should all be of practically the same proportions, and their height from ground to shoulders should approximately be the same as the length of the body from point of shoulder to rump.

NOTE.—The name Greyhound is supposed to be a corruption of Gaze hound, from its hunting by eyesight alone, but some authorities attribute it to the early British name, *Goath Hund*, "Goath" meaning "the Wind."   This the Anglo-Saxons called the *Grewhund*, since corrupted to Greyhound.

PLATE XXIII

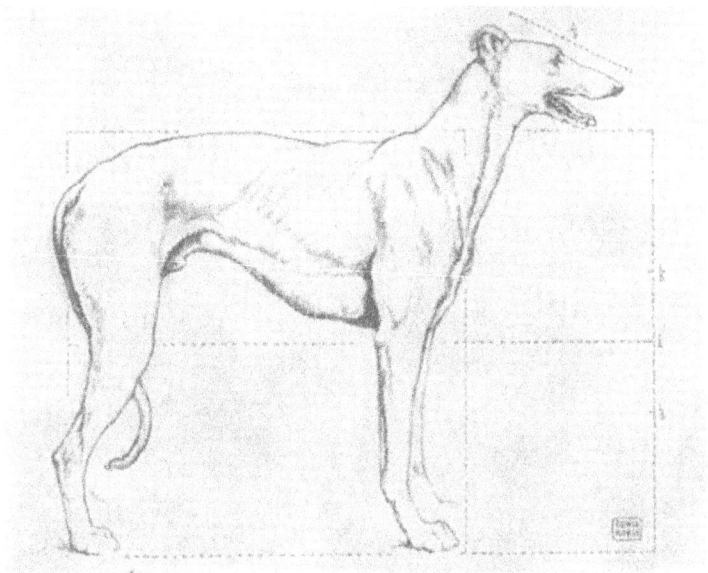

GREYHOUND

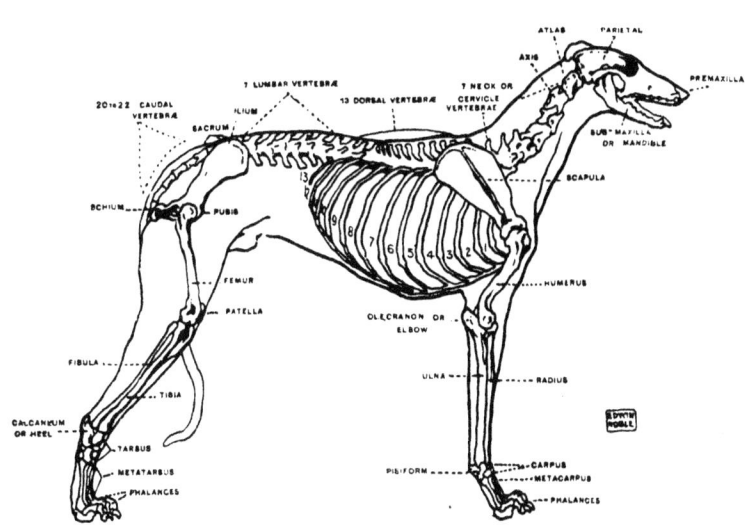

SKELETON OF A GREYHOUND

PLATE **XXIV**

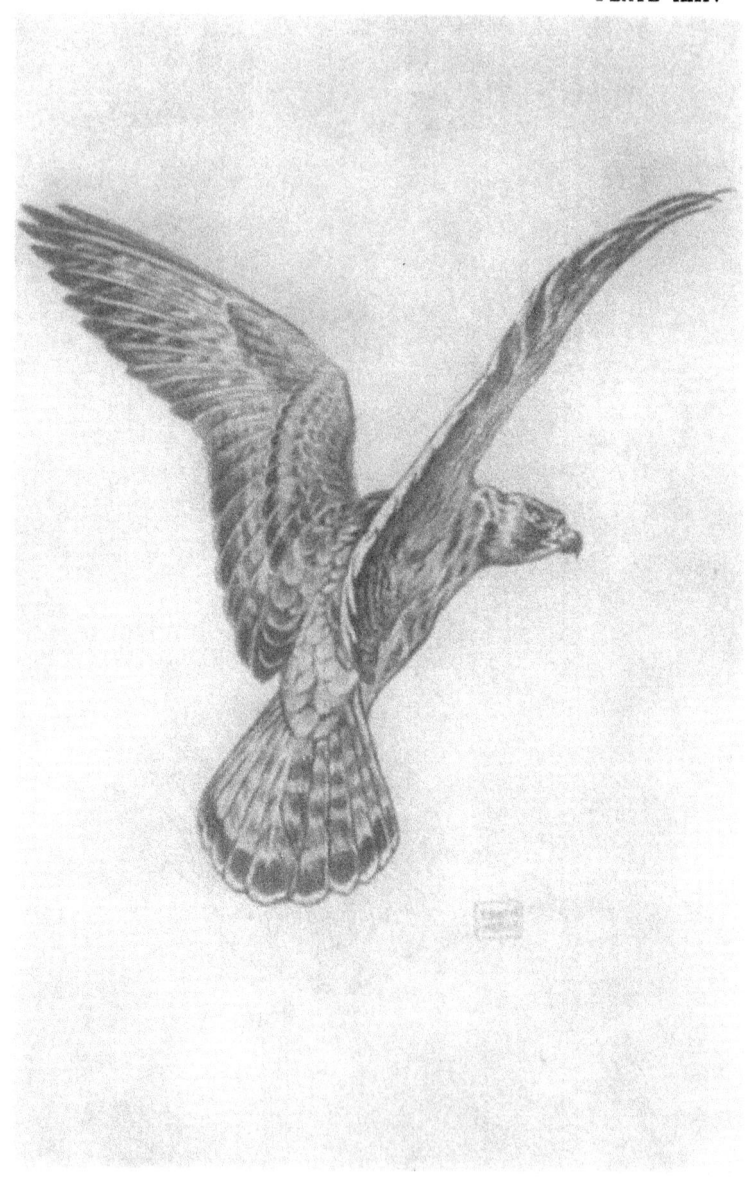

KESTREL

CHAPTER V

BIRDS

BEFORE proceeding with the anatomy, a few words upon the flight of birds will not be out of place. The first points to be recognised are that the bird is heavier than air, and, therefore, the force of gravitation drawing the body down to earth comes into play. The bird does not master the force of gravitation by mere muscular power, but by a marvellous system of planes, which enable it to float upon the currents of air. It is obvious that if a bird is to support itself by the downward blow of the wings upon the air, it must at the end of each downward stroke lift the wings upwards again, so as to prepare for the next downward movement. But each upward stroke would be in danger of neutralising the effect of the downward stroke were it not for two things—the overlap of the feathers and the convex and concave surfaces of the wings. The enormous difference this makes may be gathered if one considers the effect upon an umbrella by the wind. If the under or concave surface is exposed to the wind, the resistance is enormous as compared to the bulging or convex side, and, in a similar manner, the effort to lower the wing of a bird is so much greater as compared to the upward stroke when one realises that the wing of a bird is convex upon the upper surface and concave below. This fact is commonly overlooked by the student and painter of birds, with the result that a considerable portion of the beauty of the bird is unappreciated, namely the graceful lines of the wing (Plate xxiv).

Again, it will be noticed that the quill of the principal flight feathers is not placed exactly in the centre, and in overlapping the broader section will always be found to be underneath (Plate xxv). During a downward stroke of the wing the broad section will be pressed tightly against the narrow section of the feather above it, making one complete surface, and the passage of the air along this enables the bird to rise. The upward stroke, however, does not nullify this by bringing the bird down again, because the broad section of the feather is now unsupported and allows a certain quantity of the air to pass through the wing. Thus the muscular power of the downward stroke being so much greater almost all the muscles of flight upon a bird will be found upon the under surface of the body.

By means of the broad ligament at the base of the quills, the flight feathers can be turned at an angle in a manner similar to a Venetian blind. The action of soaring is practically that of sliding down the air until by closing the planes it once more rises, without effort, the air rushing under the convex wing.

The body of a bird is not covered thickly with feathers growing evenly from the skin. With but one or two exceptions all birds have large, bare tracts or spaces, from which feathers do not grow; these tracts in many cases, being nearly equal in the aggregate area to the feathered tracts (Plate xxvi). They are known as *Apteria*, or naked tracts, and *Pterylae*, or feather tracts. The feathers themselves vary in size and form upon each tract, and it is due to these spaces that the various movements of the bird do not cause a wrinkling or cracking of the feathers, such as is found amongst the animals.

During life the naked tracts are not visible, being covered by the overlapping feathers, but their importance to the artist lies in the fact that the groups can be clearly followed in the plumage, giving a surface modelling to what otherwise would be a globular mass of feathers.

PLATE XXV

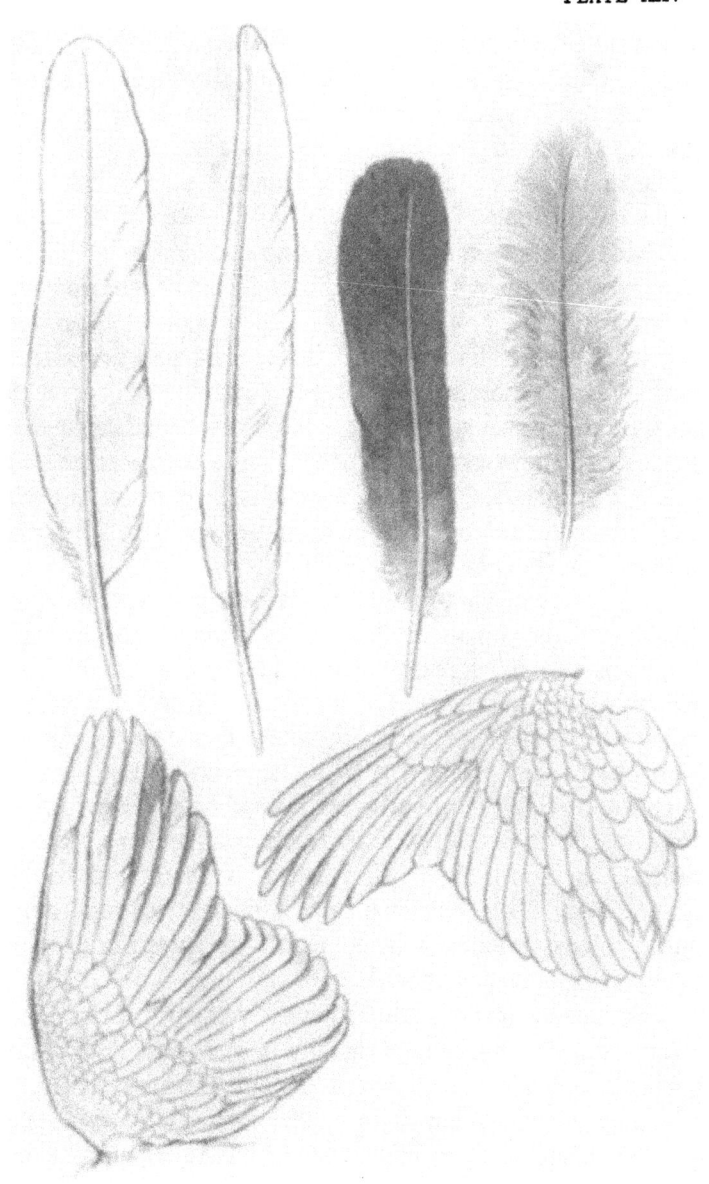

STUDIES OF FEATHERS
WINGS OF A PARTRIDGE

The sculptor, for example, by a proper appreciation of these masses, can suggest the feathering although unable to avail himself of colour or pattern, and the designer, when treating a bird in a conventional manner, can work to a clearly defined plan instead of letting the pattern become a matter of chance.

These tracts vary slightly in size and shape in different birds, but the main arrangement is all that is necessary to the artist.

Although the bones of a bird correspond to those of mankind and animals, a closer examination will show that many of them are more or less soldered together, making one solid framework, whilst others have increased in numbers.   To the artist, the skull of a bird is not a complex structure, the greater portion of it being taken up by the huge eye cavity (Plate xxvi).

This is hardly to be wondered at when it is realised that a bird depends almost for its very existence upon its sight, either for safety or food.   In connection with this, it is interesting to note that nearly all birds of prey have the eyes placed well in front of the skull, whilst those that are preyed upon have them placed on either side where they can see all round them.   Compare the Hawk or the Owl with a Pigeon or a Sparrow, and the same rule, when applied to animals, the Rabbit and the Mouse, compared to the Cat and the Fox.   The eye of a bird is perfectly round and is usually black, encircled by a highly coloured iris, which contracts or enlarges at will.

The faculty of focus adjustment is very highly developed to accommodate the almost instantaneous changes of vision. A Hawk soaring like a speck in the blue sky minutely watching every movement upon the earth below, makes his deadly plunge with unerring aim.   A Woodcock avoids every obstacle in the thickest coppice whilst travelling at a tremendous speed, and a Pigeon or a Sparrow whilst pecking up the crumbs from the ground, can watch every

PLATE XXVI

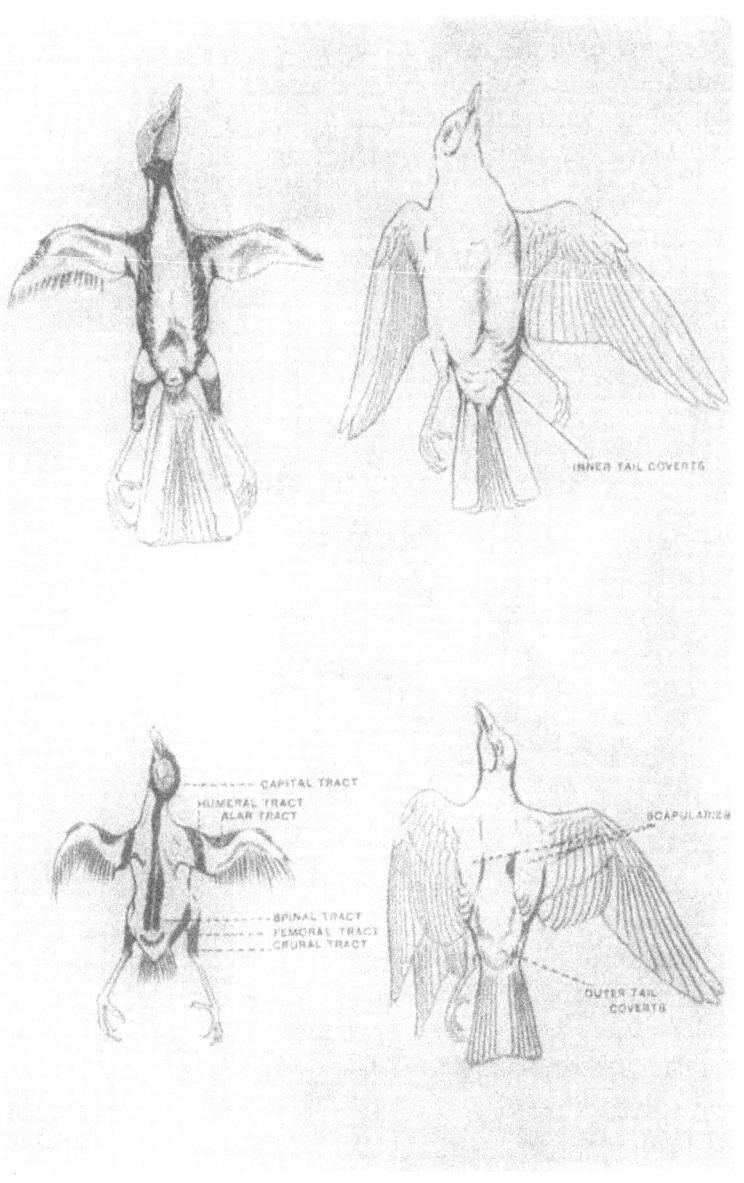

FEATHER TRACTS OF BIRDS

59

movement of the prowling cat or overhead hawk. The
eye of the Owl is specially adapted for nocturnal use ; the
radiation of the feathers and the series of bony plates con-
centrating the vision, although, in addition, this bird
possesses a very acute sense of hearing.

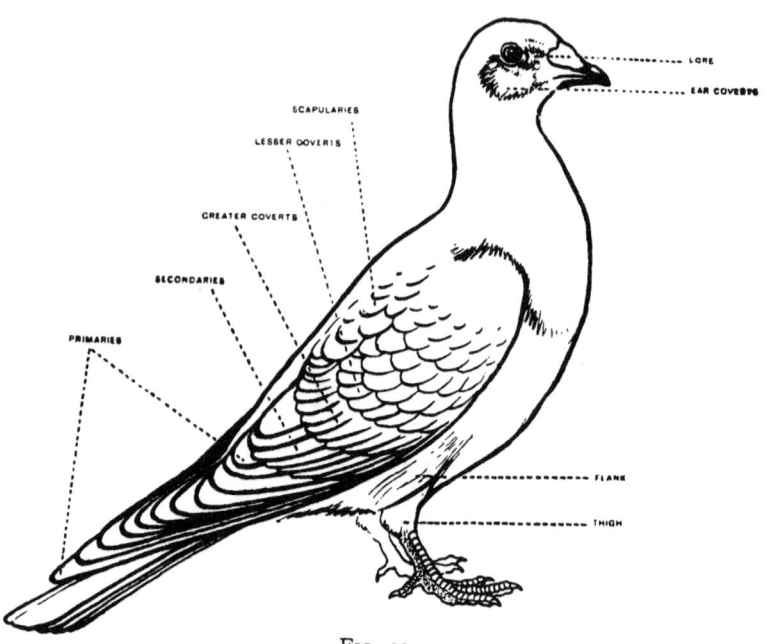

FIG. 29.
FEATHERS OF A PIGEON

The bird has three eyelids, upper and lower and nictitating membrane. When sleepy, the lower eyelid almost
covers the eyeball, in contrast to the human eye wherein the
upper lid possesses the greater movement, but when wink-
ing the bird draws the nictitating membrane across the
eyeball. This membrane, or third lid, is semi-transparent
and dilutes the intense glare whilst enabling it to see plainly,
and is undoubtedly made use of when facing the light of
the sun.

Another safeguard possessed by the bird alone is the power of turning the neck farther round than is possible to either mankind or animals. This faculty is owing to two causes—firstly, at the base of the skull will be found a small knob which fits into the first vertebræ of the neck

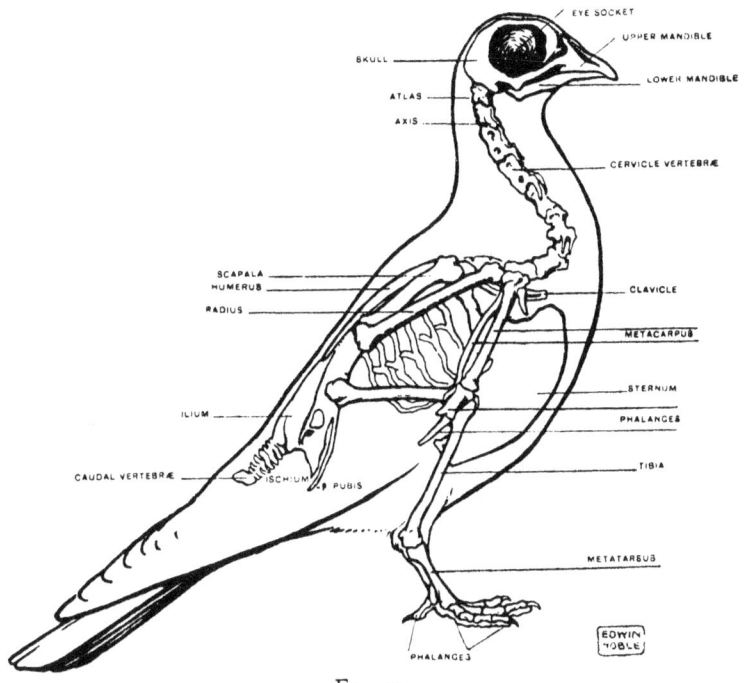

FIG. 30.
SKELETON OF A PIGEON

and serves as a single pivot, whilst all other animals possess two projections, one on either side; and secondly, the increase in the number of *Cervicle Vertebræ* (Plate XXVI). The long neck of the Giraffe only contains seven neck-bones, whilst the Sparrow possesses fourteen, and the Swan as many as twenty-three, and this flexibility on the part of the bird enables it to reach any part of its plumage. The remainder of the *Vertebræ* on the contrary have become fused in such a

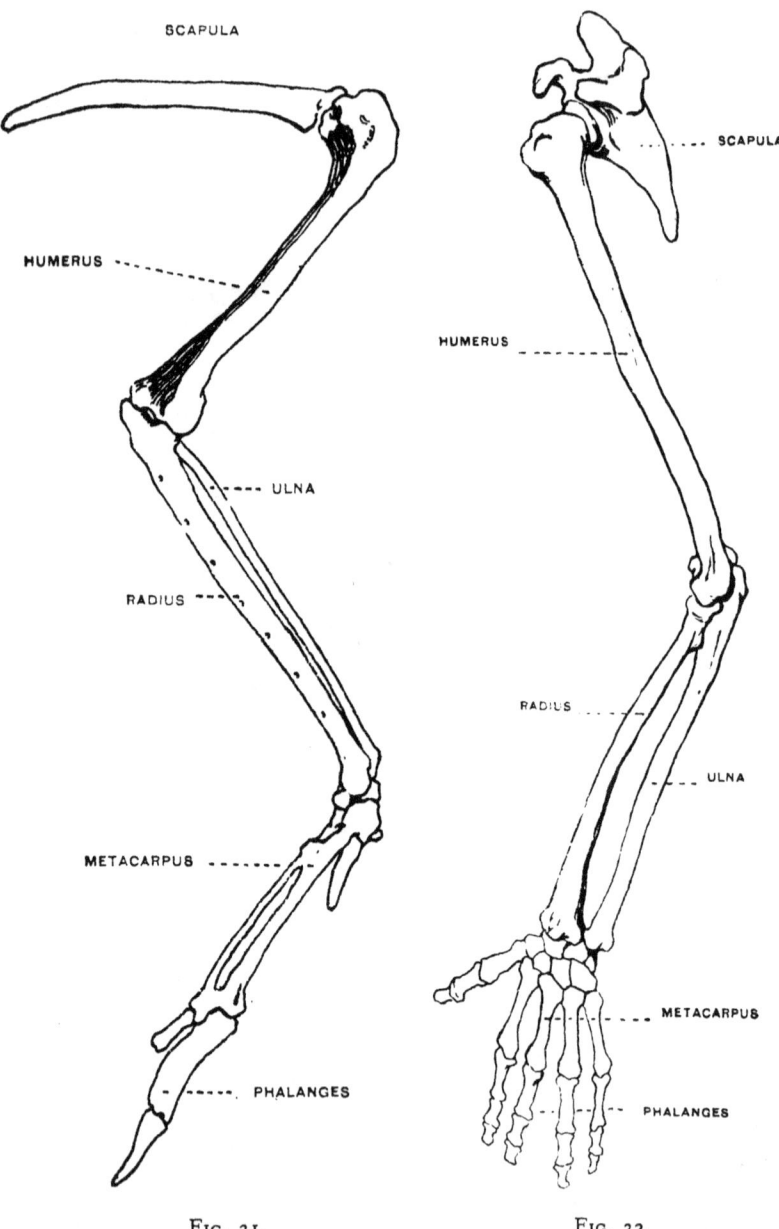

SCAPULA

HUMERUS

ULNA

RADIUS

METACARPUS

PHALANGES

SCAPULA

HUMERUS

RADIUS

ULNA

METACARPUS

PHALANGES

FIG. 31.
WING OF A BIRD

FIG. 32.
ARM OF A MAN

PLATE XXVII

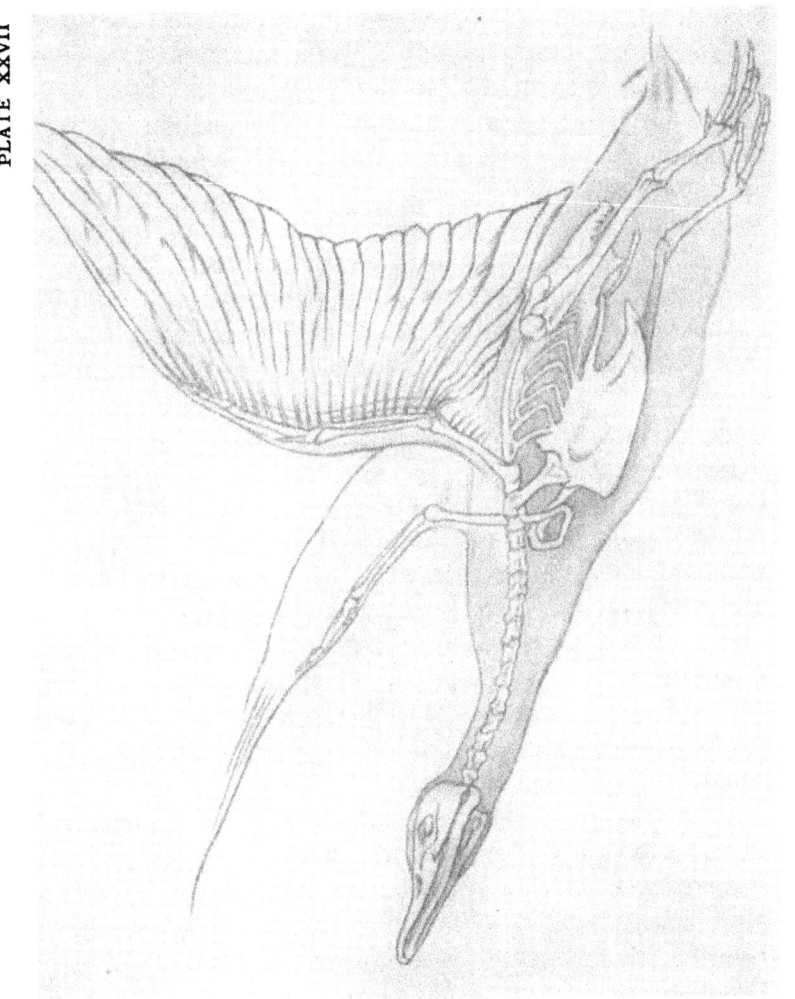

SKELETON OF A WILD DUCK IN FLIGHT

manner as to be practically one bone, with corresponding lack of movement.   In a bird almost the entire muscular power is devoted to the powers of flight, and as the greater the muscle the more powerful must be the bone to which it attaches, consequently we find a considerable increase in the size of the bones to which the wing muscles are attached. The great flight muscles, or *Pectoral* muscles, form the breast, and these lie on either side of a strong keel dividing the *Sternum* or breastbone.   The shape of the keel varies in nearly every species of bird, having the greatest development in those of powerful flight, whilst in those who have lost the use of their wings the keel has disappeared entirely, and the *Sternum* is a flat plate, similar to that of the human skeleton.   Many powerful birds of flight do not, however, use an extraordinary amount of muscular power.   They soar and float upon the air currents, making use of the feathers of the wing to act as a series of planes, and the gulls and the Albatross have comparatively small keels to the *Sternum* by comparison with a Pigeon, and the latter again is small compared to that of a Humming Bird.   The movement of the wings of this small bird is so fast that they appear to be transparent, and it has been estimated that they make from 600 to 1,000 strokes of the wing per minute, developing more muscular energy than any other animal.

It will be noted that the *Sternum* of animals is attached to the ribs only.   In the bird, these latter have been strengthened by a bony projection from each rib overlapping the next behind it, forming a kind of basket work. Even so, the constant pressure of the chest muscles during flight are apt to cause undue contraction were it not for the additional support given by a stout column of bone called the *Coracoid Bone*.   Attached to this again is the *Clavicle*, better known as the Merrythought.   It will thus be found that the shoulder of a bird has two bones which are not present in animals, whilst the *Scapula*, or shoulder-blade

PLATE XXVIII

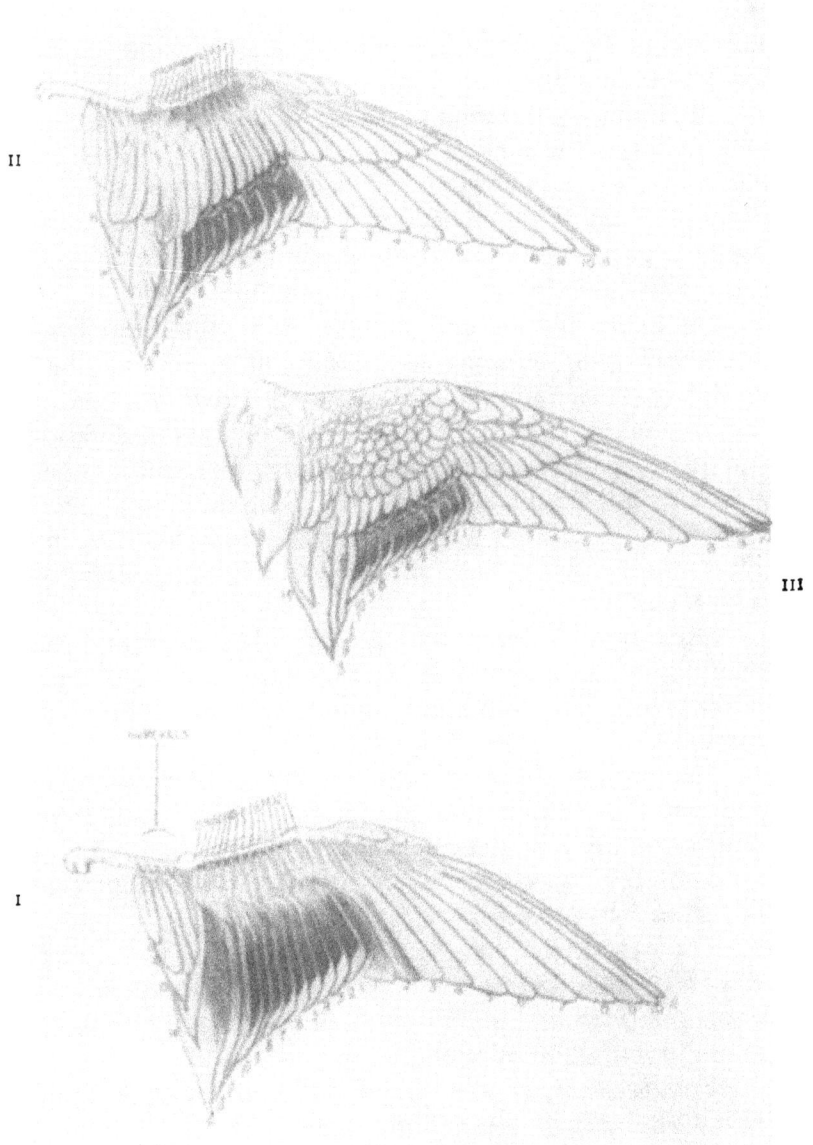

WING OF WILD DUCK

I. PRIMARIES AND SECONDARIES II. GREATER COVERTS
III. LESSER COVERTS

itself, takes a very secondary place, being the long knife-like bone lying alongside the *Dorsal Vertebræ*.

The similarity between the wing of a bird and the arm of a man is very marked (Figs. 31 and 32), the greatest change taking place at the wrist where two bones take the place of eight. The fourth and fifth fingers have also disappeared, so that the bird has the first and second finger joined together, and a vestige of the thumb.

The *Ilium, Ischium,* and *Pubis* have become fused into one bone, along with the vertebræ; and the *Femur* bone of the leg is relatively short. The knee proper of a bird is seldom visible, even in such long-legged birds as Herons and Flamingos, where the extra length is due to the elongation of the next two joints, the *Tibia* and the *Tarsus*. The so-called knee of a bird is actually the heel, and the *Tarsus* bones have become merged into one shank covered with scales.

In the foot, the great toe has turned backward, and the small toe has completely disappeared—the bird thus walking upon its toes and not upon the flat of the foot as in mankind.

The large feathers of the wing with slightly tapering ends are the Primaries, or first flight feathers, and those with broad ends are the Secondaries.

Although apparently very complicated, the arrangement of feathers on a wing is quite easy to follow.

The first *Primary* feather grows from the first joint, extending as a continuation of that bone. From the second bone, two Primary feathers grow, and from the next bone either seven, eight, or nine.

The Secondaries grow from the *Radius*, and average about fourteen in the smaller birds. These are always known as the flight feathers of a wing.

NOTE.—Primaries (Plate xxviii) vary but little in number, usually nine, ten, or eleven. Secondaries on the contrary vary considerably. In such birds wherein the

PLATE XXIX

(a)

(b)

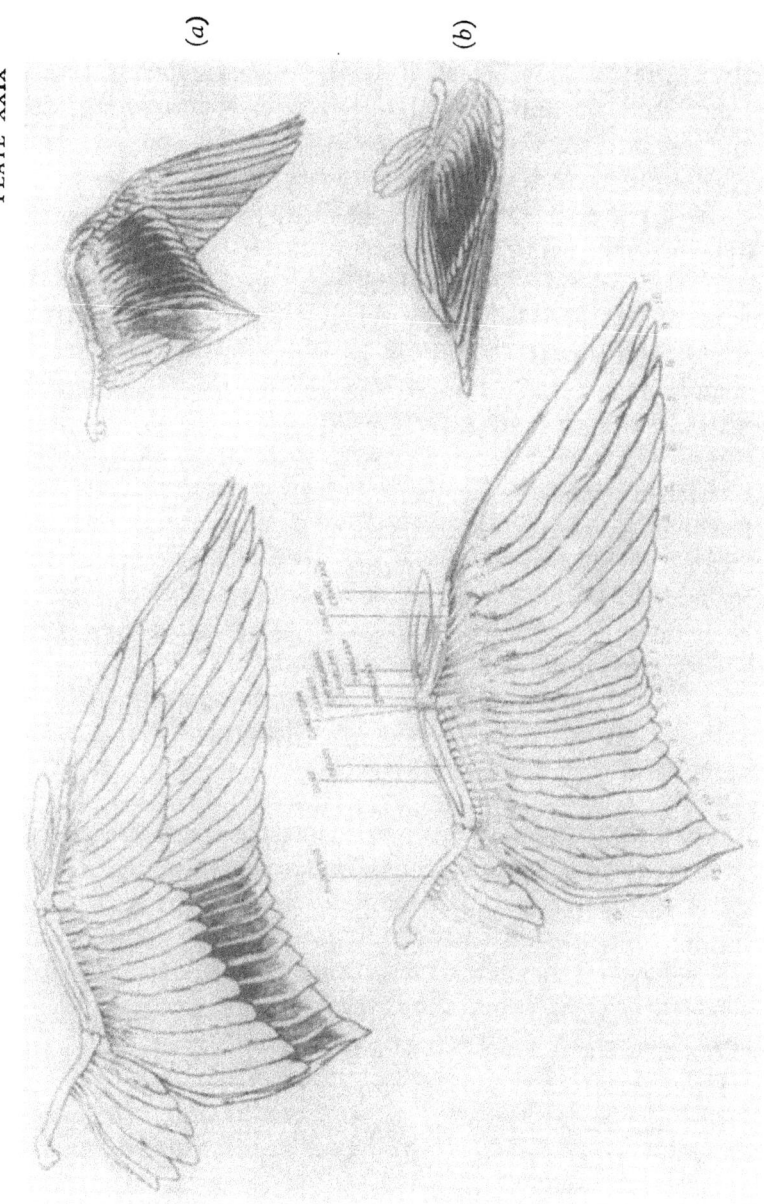

UNDERSIDE OF THE WING OF A WILD DUCK
(a) SHOWING ACTION OF CLOSING WING

wing is greatly lengthened it is the Secondaries which are increased in numbers, the two extremes being the Humming Bird with ten Primaries and six Secondaries, and the Albatross, with ten Primaries and forty Secondaries.

It is obvious that if these flight feathers were not supported in some manner, the pressure of air in a stroke of the wing would cause them to bend at the base of the quill. This is safeguarded against by a broad ligament, through which the quills pass, helping to keep the feathers in position, and again by a second row of stiff feathers, reaching about half way. They grow immediately over the flight feathers, so close that the two seem to have grown together and attach to the same ligament. Consequently, they are identical in numbers to the feathers they cover, and are known as the Greater Coverts, the under surface of the wing being supported in the same manner. Overlapping these again will be found the Lesser Coverts, usually about five rows, each row reversing in direction.

NOTE.—A peculiarity about the smaller song-birds is that they seldom have more than three rows of Lesser Coverts, and often these three rows never properly develop.

Five short stiff feathers grow from the Thumb, and are known as the Bastard wing. The *Penna* are again a series of short stiff feathers, and help to close the gap between the body of the bird and the innermost feathers of the arm or Secondaries. In birds, such as the Gull tribe, where the *Humerus* is very long, these feathers are large and well-developed. They grow in a double series, one from the upper and one from the under surface of the bone.

From the *Scapula* grow a clearly defined group of feathers, which act as a roof, overlapping both the body of the bird and the upper portion of the wing when closed. Consequently, when a bird is at rest and the wing pressed to the body, it is impossible for rain or moisture to trickle down inside the wing.

PLATE XXX

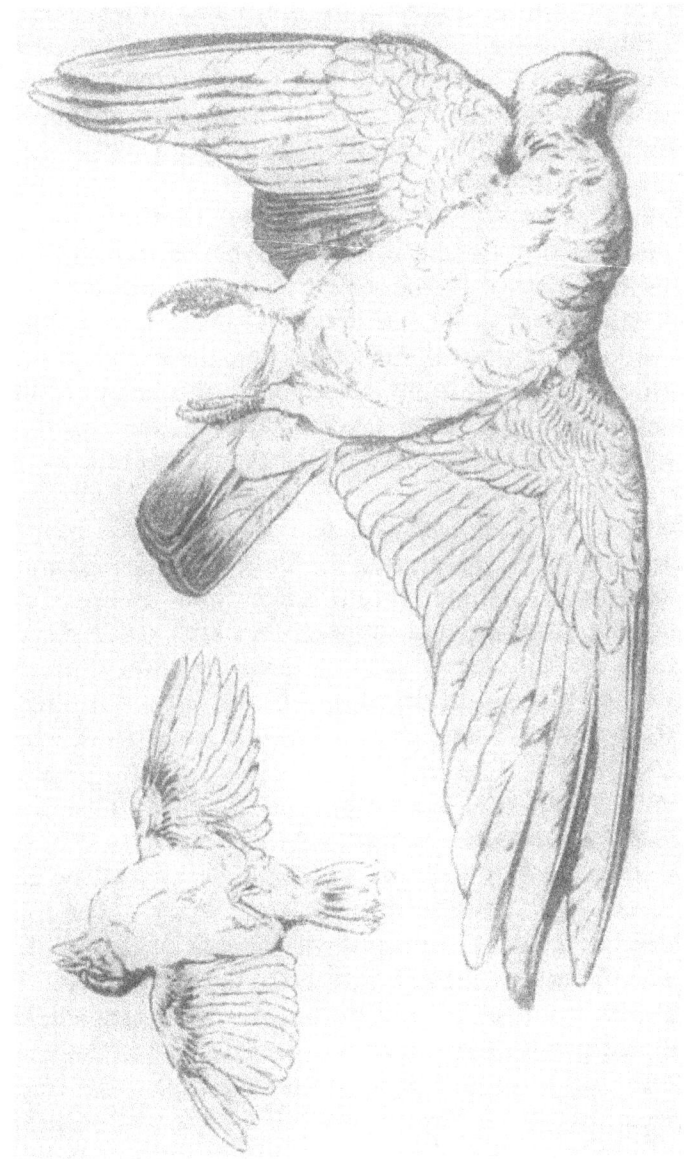

WING OF A WOOD PIGEON

WING OF A YOUNG SPARROW
(UNDERSIDE)

NOTE.—Upon alighting, the first action of a bird is to settle the wings comfortably against the body and beneath this group of feathers. Most small birds require to seek shelter during rain, the *Scapularies* not being well developed, but in all water birds, also the Eagles and Hawks, their shape and pattern is very marked.

The feathers of the breast, known as the plumage feathers, vary considerably in different types of birds. From this part of the body the down feathers grow, and are found most highly developed in the Heron tribe, where they form large patches over the breast and thighs, known as "Powder down." If carefully examined, this will be found to consist of a number of feather barbs matted together, and of such a friable nature that they disintegrate at the touch into a fine powder.

In some birds, *Filo-Plumes* play a conspicuous part in the colouration of the plumage. They attain great length and form large patches, as in the white thigh patches of the Cormorant, or give a hoary appearance to the necks of such birds as the Condor Vulture. Little is known of the meaning or use of Filo-Plumes. They are the long hair-like threads which remain over the body of a fowl when plucked.

Many of the Contour feathers are double. That is to say, they have an aftershaft known as *Hyporhachis*. In the Emu, the aftershaft is the same length as the feather, and it is always well developed in the game birds. The long plume-like feathers growing down the back of these latter, and also the domestic fowl are formed in this manner.

The first aim of the artist or designer when introducing a bird in flight is to introduce a beautiful shape to the wing contour, and so often this is done at the expense of truth, ignoring the fact that every type of bird has its distinctive form of wing. A bird which spends the greater part of its life in the air, such as the Swallow, has a wing in the form of a long, narrow-pointed blade. Whilst in those

PLATE XXXI

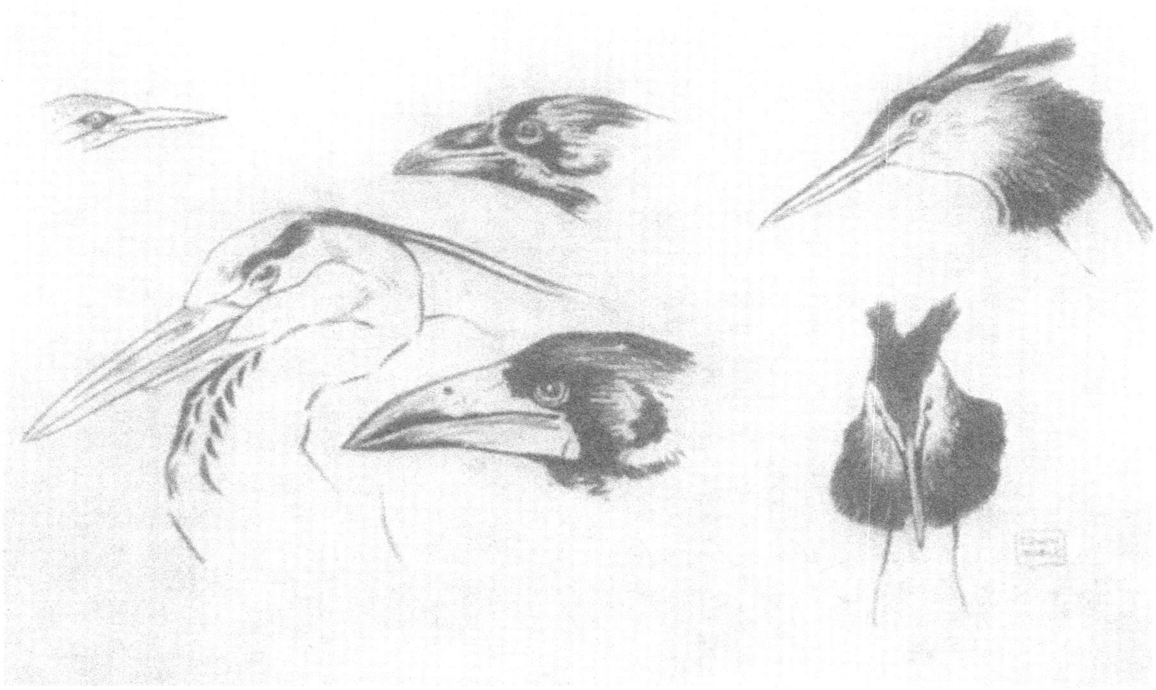

BEAKS. DAGGER TYPES

1. KINGFISHER   2. RAVEN: SHOWING FEATHERS UPON BEAK
3 AND 6. GREBE   4. HERON
5. ROOK. WITHOUT FEATHERS UPON BEAK

that fly but short distances, such as the Partridge, the wing takes a broad, rounded shape, and there is an infinite variety between these two extremes.

The importance of this cannot be over-estimated by figure painters when introducing angels, cherubs, or evil spirits into their designs. A wing ill-designed and with loose feathers as if in moult is constantly seen in sculptures and designs, when a more decorative result, artistically, would have been gained by a true form of wing. Imagination hesitates at the thought of angels fluttering about with the short quick action of a Sparrow, whilst the spirits of the wind should surely hurl themselves through space with the sinister knife-like wing.

The typical form is ten Primaries of equal length, but owing to manner of attachment the first feathers appear to be the longer, whilst the remainder appear to diminish. In birds which fly with remarkable rapidity, that is, with rapid strokes of the wing, including the song birds without exception, the second feather is the longest and the first feather abbreviated.

The beak of a bird has a greater scientific than artistic interest ; its many variations being adaptations to different methods of feeding. The earliest known fossil birds were provided with teeth, but modern birds have a sheath composed of horn, and in accordance with the nature of the food, the shape of the sheath or beak varies.

The common form is the Dagger type, serving in addition as a hammer, pair of pincers, or instrument for holding or tearing. Beaks such as this are possessed by the Raven, the Rook, the Kingfisher, and the Finch tribe. More specialised types are found in the Herons and Egrets, with, in addition, an arrangement of the muscles of the *Cervicle Vertebra*, which enables the head to be darted forward with lightning speed, and so spear or transfix the prey.

PLATE XXXII

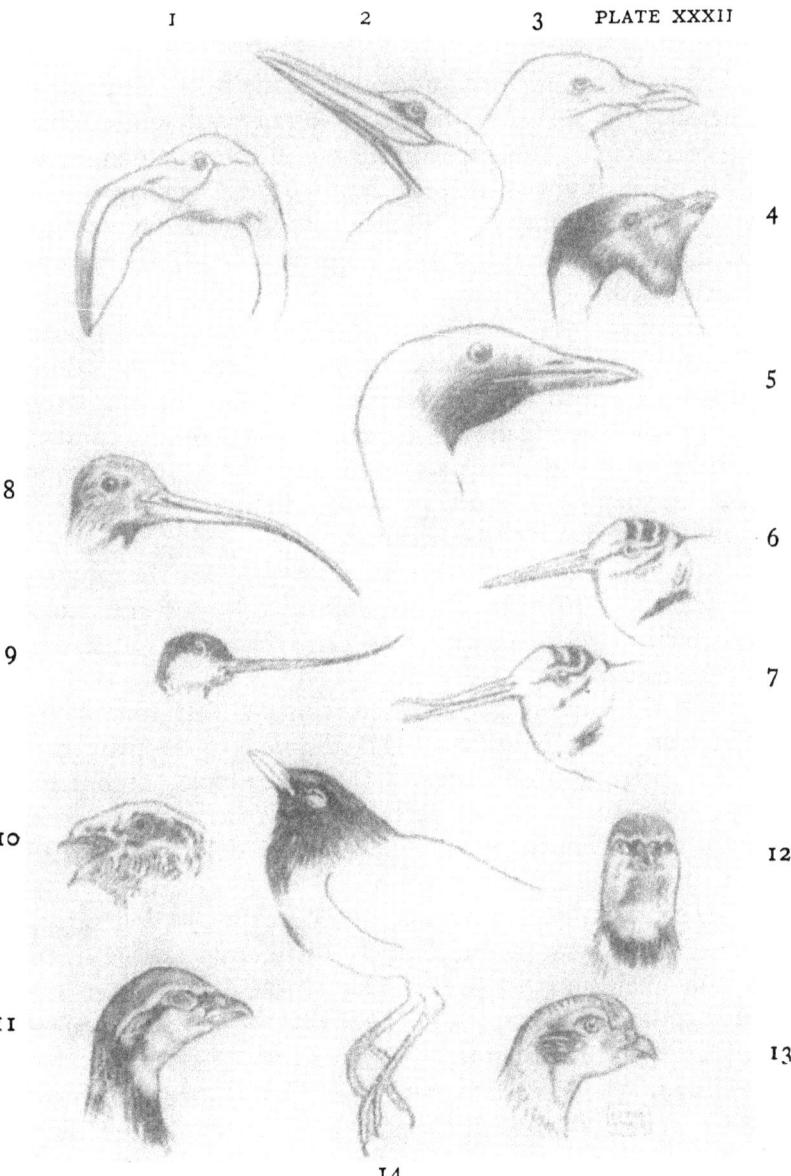

BEAKS, PROBES, FISH-EATING TYPES, ETC.

1. FLAMINGO	8. CURLEW
2. GANNET	9. AVOCET
3. GULL	10. NIGHTJAR
4. PENGUIN	11 AND 12. FRENCH PARTRIDGE
5. DIVER	13. BRITISH PARTRIDGE
6. WOODCOCK	14. BLACKBIRD

7. WOODCOCK. SHOWING MOVEMENT OF BEAK IN ACT OF SEIZING A WORM

Birds with this development carry the head with a distinct angular curve to the neck—totally different to the curves taken by the neck of a Swan, Crane, or Flamingo. A Heron in flight carries the head curved back upon the shoulders in complete contrast to a bird similar in build, such as the Stork, where the head is carried outstretched.

Certain forms of beaks have developed to become probes for use in soft mud, examples being the Curlew, the Snipe, the Avocet, and the Woodcock. The beak of the latter has a mobile tip, which is extremely sensitive, and on contact with a worm can grasp and withdraw same from a considerable depth of mud with the minimum amount of effort to the slender beak itself.

Very few birds use the feet to convey food to the mouth, but this is done by the Parrots, whose beak is of the pincer type only. In exchange, these birds make as much use of the beak in climbing as of their feet.

The Ducks have a specialised form of beak, suitable to their methods of feeding. The inner edges are provided with rows of small plates, almost like teeth, and their function is to act as strainers, the water being forced out by the movement of the tongue whilst the small animalculae and particles of food are retained.

The fish-eating ducks, like the other fish-eating birds, are provided with a small hook at the end to enable them to hold their slippery prey, and a greater development of this is found in the beaks of the birds of prey, although in the latter its use is more for the purpose of tearing and rending. The feet are in these birds the weapons of offence, being provided with powerful talons, but they are also used to hold down the food whilst tearing it to pieces. Both the Crows and the Vultures hold down their food by means of the feet.

The beak of the grain eaters is usually softer in structure and slightly curved, whilst the Swallows and similar insect

PLATE XXXIII

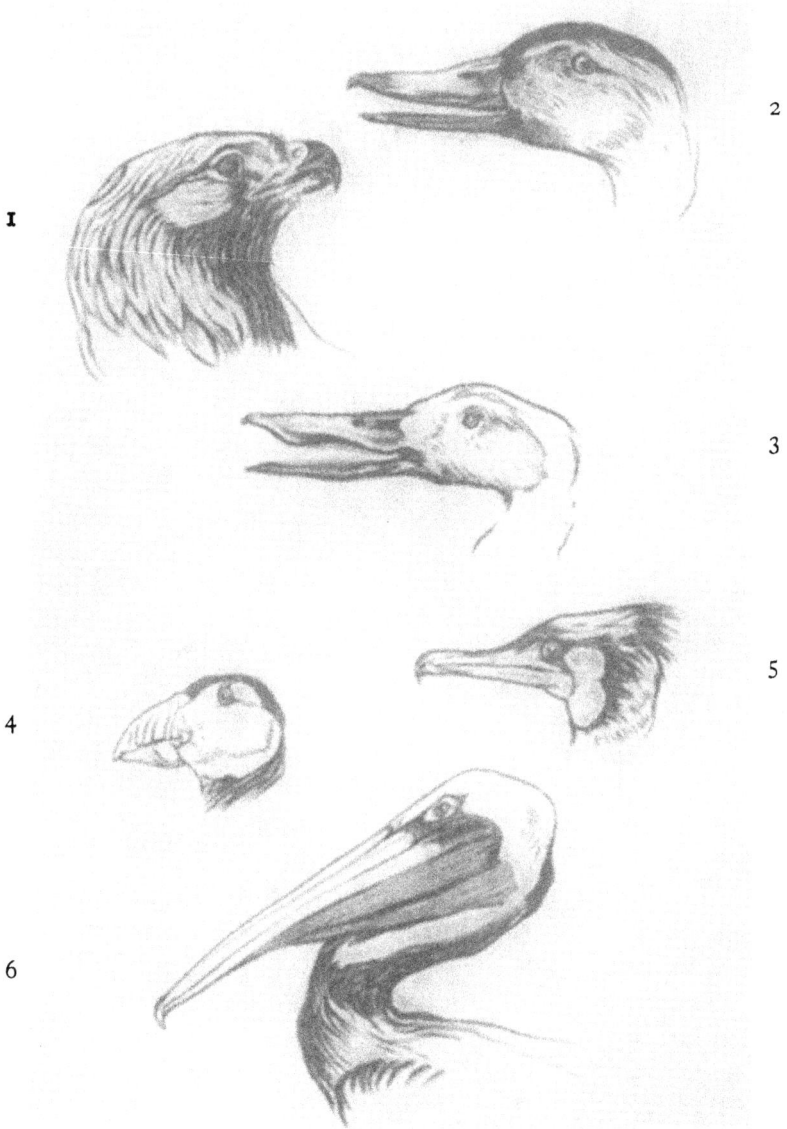

BEAKS OF BIRDS
Birds of Prey, Ducks and Fish-eating Types

1. Golden Eagle	2. Duck	3. Shoveller Duck
4. Penguin	5. Cormorant	6. Pelican

eating birds have extremely short beaks with very wide mouths or gape, which enables them to snap and swallow immediately whilst in full flight. The mouth of the Nightjar is fringed with bristles to brush off the wings of the night moths, whilst the succulent body-part is being swallowed.

Perhaps no greater scope for decorative treatment exists than in the feet of birds (Plates xxxiv, xxxv, xxxvi), and perhaps no greater failure to make the most of the opportunity is more evident.

The foot of every bird is covered with scales, the pattern of which is a delight in itself, and yet how seldom is this fact made use of for the purpose of design. For the painter of pictures there is some excuse for the neglect, because his problems are those of tone values and colour, and the details have often to be sacrificed for the sake of breadth, but the student who wishes to treat the bird in pen and ink or other decorative manner, cannot afford to overlook this pattern.

The principal laws governing the structural formation of the foot are :—

The first toe corresponding to the human thumb is placed at the back and consists of one bone only.

The second toe is on the inside of the foot and consists of two bones.

The third or middle toe consists of three bones, and the Fourth or outer toe has four bones. With very few exceptions does this rule vary.

The Passerenes or Perching birds (Plate xxxiv) have the hind toe long, and freely movable to enable them to grasp the bough, and the method of progression upon ground is usually to hop.

The Walking birds (Plate xxxiv), such as Fowls, Game birds, etc., have the hind toe small, often not reaching the ground, and practically without movement, whilst in the Ducks this toe is almost negligible.

PLATE XXXIV

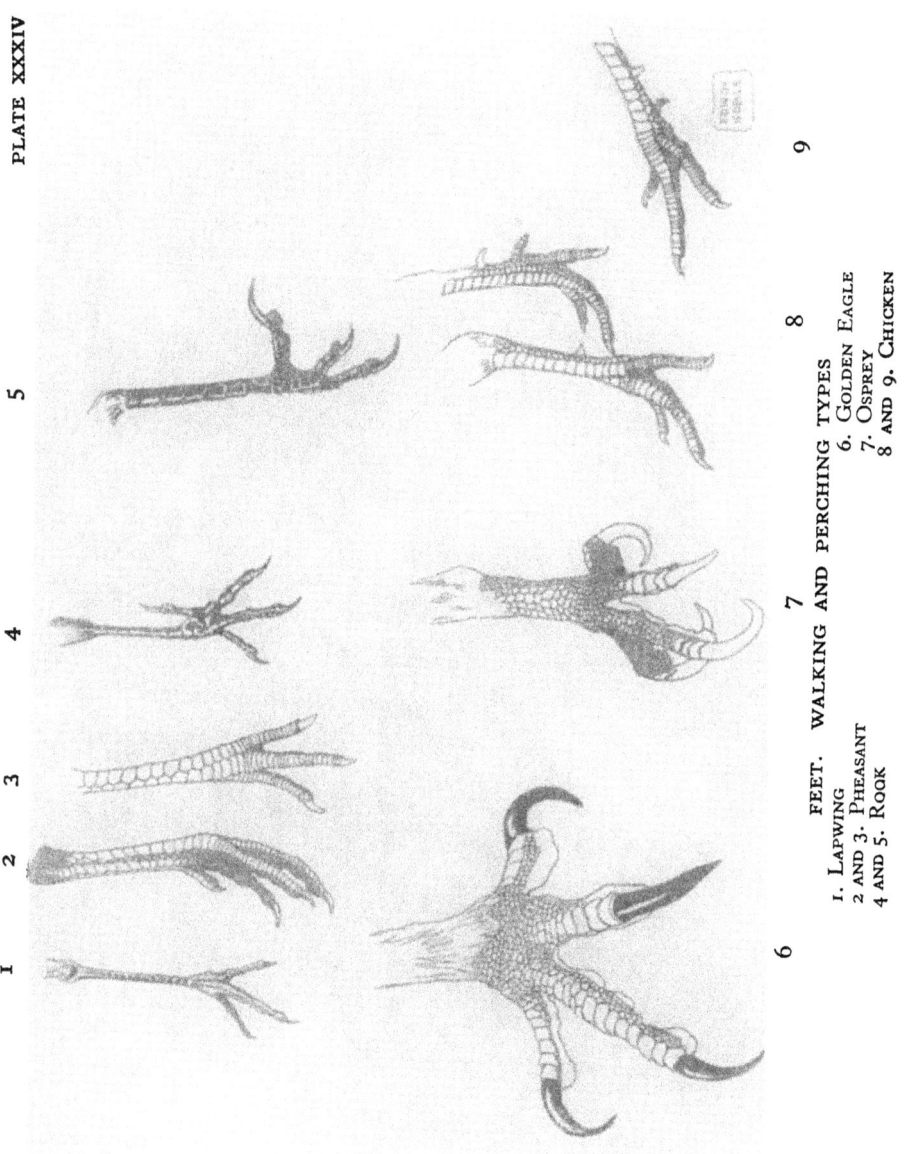

FEET. WALKING AND PERCHING TYPES

1. LAPWING
2 AND 3. PHEASANT
4 AND 5. ROOK
6. GOLDEN EAGLE
7. OSPREY
8 AND 9. CHICKEN

PLATE XXXV

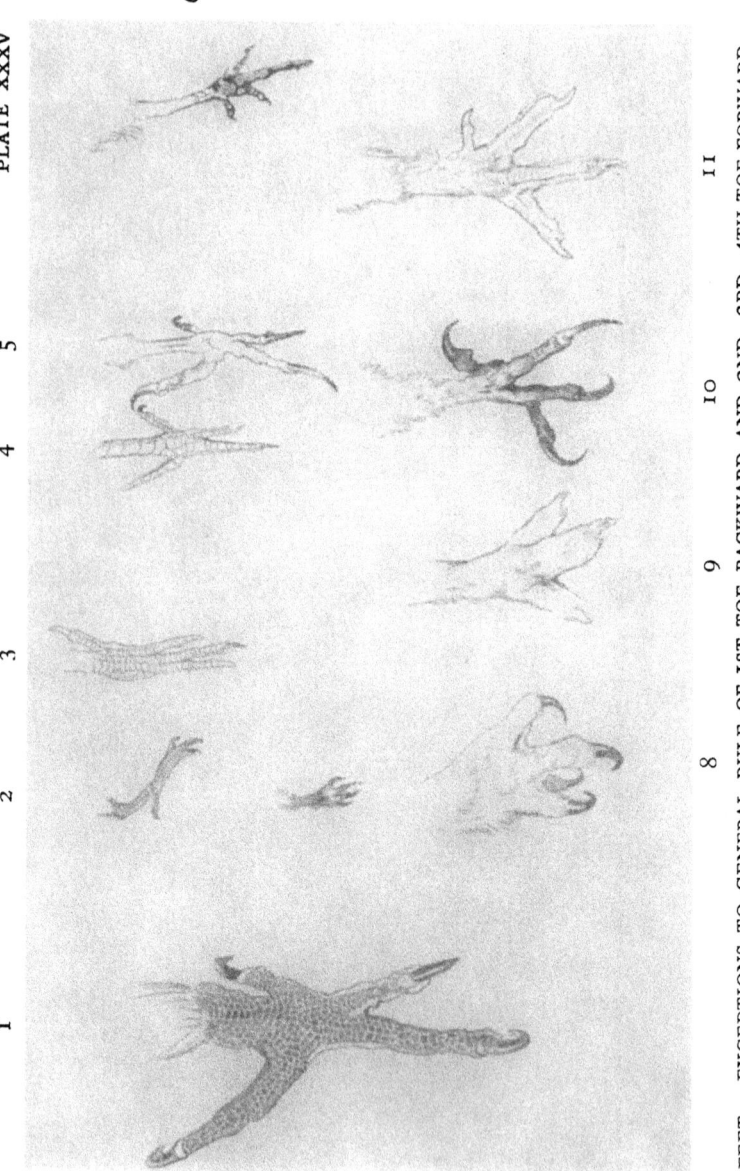

FEET. EXCEPTIONS TO GENERAL RULE OF 1ST TOE BACKWARD AND 2ND, 3RD, 4TH TOE FORWARD

1. PARROT (ZYGODACTYLE)
2 AND 3. KINGFISHER (SYNDACTYLE)
4 AND 5. CUCKOO (ZYGODACTYLE)
6. GOATSUCKER. SHOWING COMB UPON 3RD TOE
7. SWIFT. ALL TOES IN FRONT

8. OWL. TOES IN PAIRS
9. PTARMIGAN. TOES FEATHERED
10. BARN OWL. SHOWING REVERSIBLE 4TH TOE
     AND SERRATED 3RD TOE
11. GROUSE. TOES FEATHERED

PLATE XXXVI

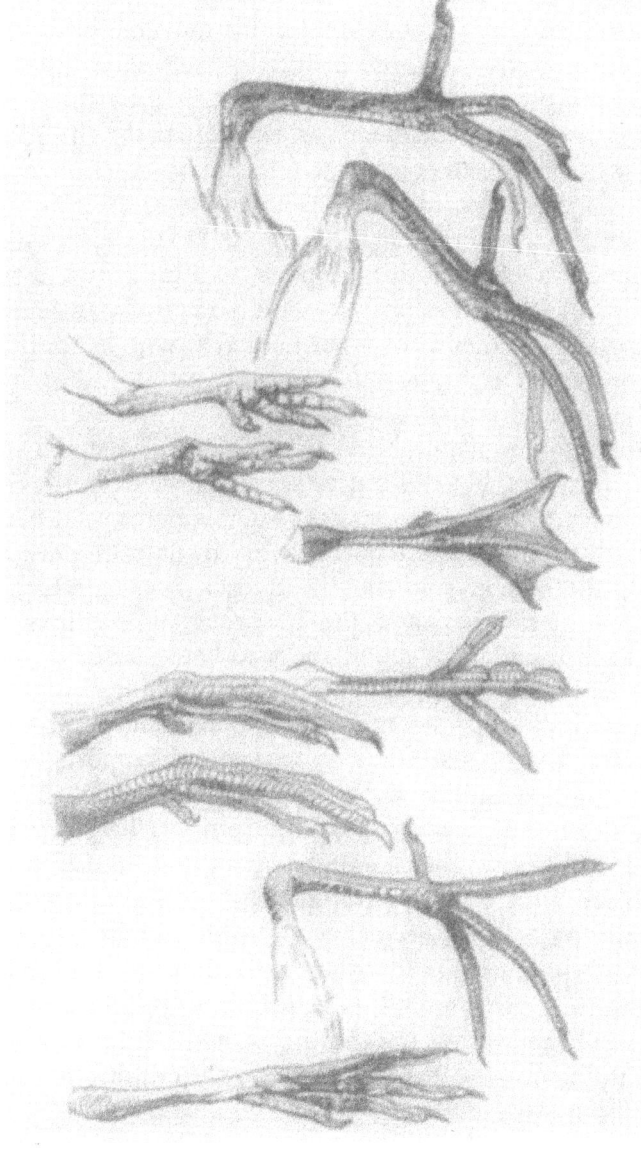

FEET. TYPES OF WADING BIRDS, SHOWING THE PATTERN FORMED BY THE SCALES

1. MOORHEN
2. PINTAIL DUCK

3. PARTRIDGE
4. MOORHEN
7. MOORHEN

5. COOT
6. PINTAIL DUCK

The Birds of Prey on the contrary have this toe very developed, and capable of considerable movement.

In some birds the three front toes are joined together throughout the greater part of their length, without any separate movement whatever ; an example being the Kingfisher, who uses the feet for perching and no other purpose, and is known as *Syndactyle*.

Many of the climbing birds (Plate xxxv), such as the Woodpeckers, have the toes in pairs, two in front and two behind, and the Parrot possesses the power of transferring the second toe either in front or behind at will, hence these feet are known as *Zygodactyle*.

The Cuckoo is also *Zygodactyle*.

Most of the Water birds (Plate xxxvi) have the toes joined by a web, but this varies considerably from the foot of a Pelican, wherein all four toes are joined for their entire length, the Duck wherein the three front toes only are joined, the Grebe and the Coot, each toe of which is provided with lobes, and the Moorhen, whose toes are remarkably long and slender, the web being nothing more than a flattening of the under surface of the toe.

The Swallow passes the greater part of its life on the wing, and has no use for legs except for supports when resting. Consequently these have become so small that the bird has a difficulty in rising from the level ground should it by any chance alight thereon. It prefers to launch itself into the air from the eaves, roof-tops, or telegraph wires, and the toes have become of little service except to cling, consequently the four toes are all in front.

Like most other animals whose habitat is ice and snow, the foot of the Ptarmigan is feathered upon the sole, whilst the toes themselves, for the sake of warmth, are covered throughout with feathers.

There is one law, without any exception whatever, governing the arrangement of feathers in the tail of a bird.

PLATE XXXVII

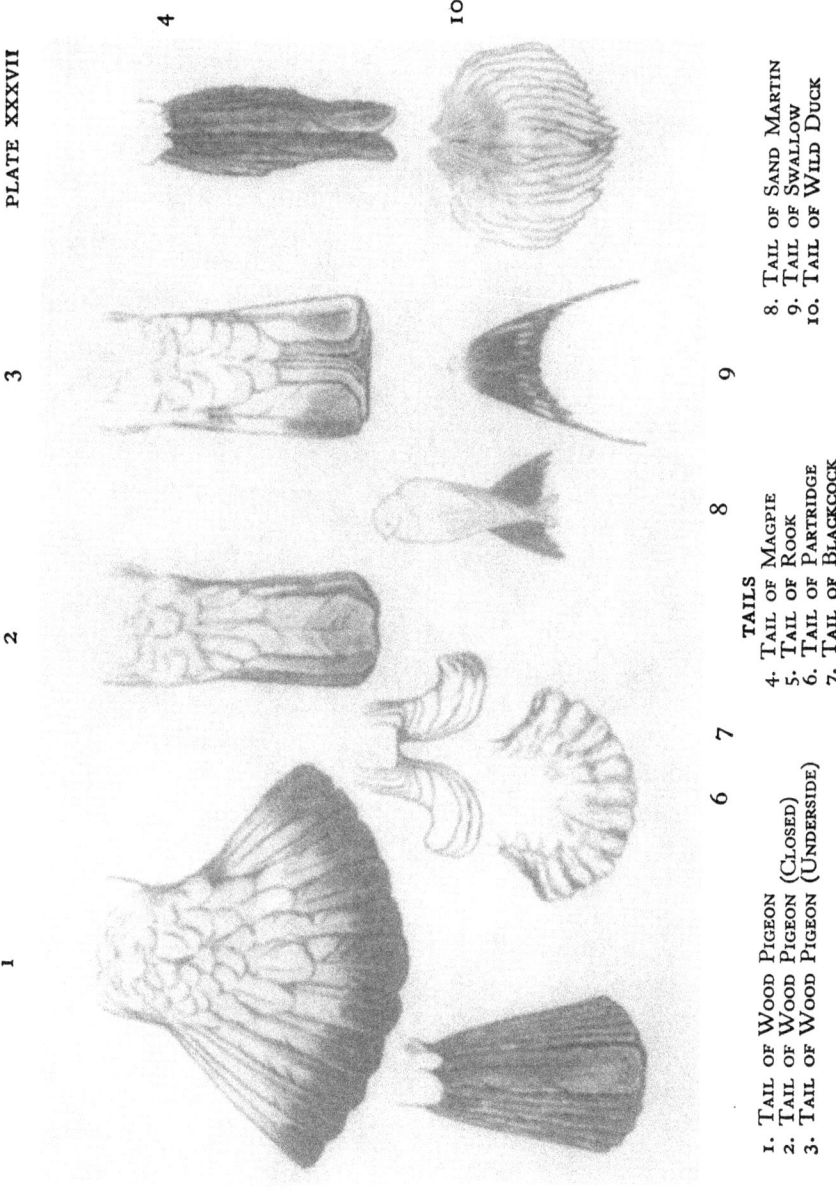

TAILS

1. Tail of Wood Pigeon
2. Tail of Wood Pigeon (Closed)
3. Tail of Wood Pigeon (Underside)
4. Tail of Magpie
5. Tail of Rook
6. Tail of Partridge
7. Tail of Blackcock
8. Tail of Sand Martin
9. Tail of Swallow
10. Tail of Wild Duck

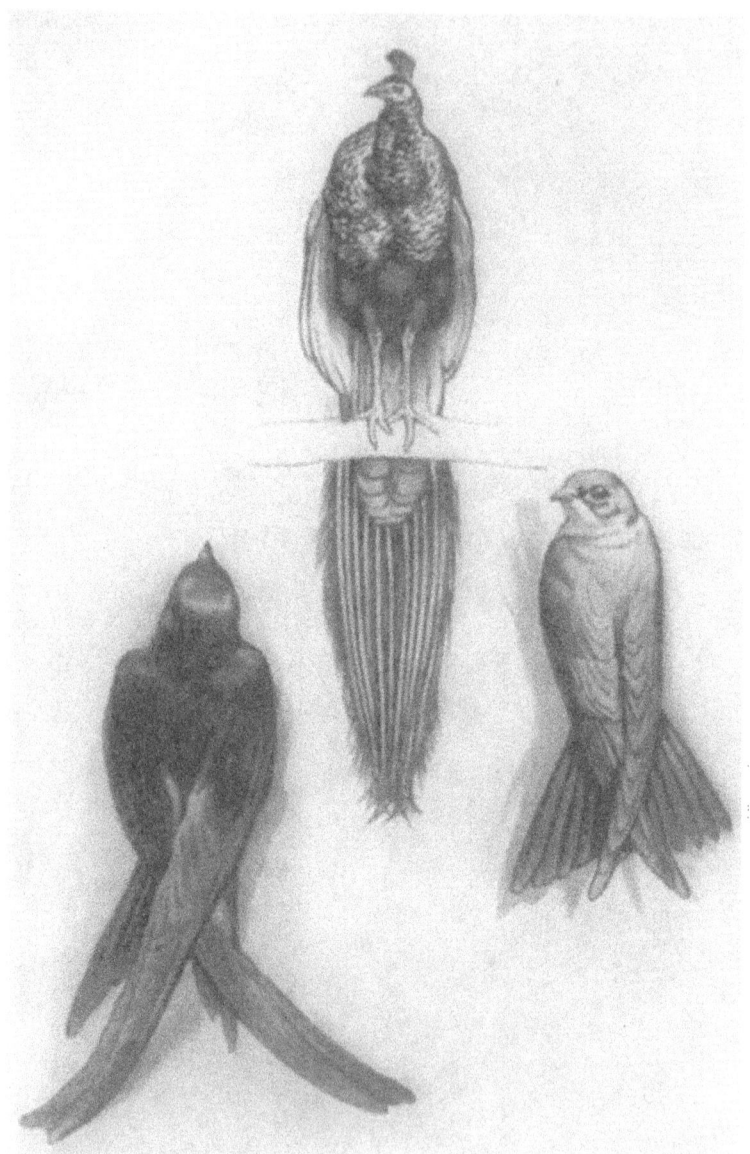

2

3

1. PEACOCK, SHOWING REAL TAIL BENEATH THE SO-CALLED TAIL
2. SWALLOW, SHOWING METHOD OF CLINGING TO WALL BY AID
OF WINGS
3. MARTIN, SHOWING METHOD OF CLINGING TO WALL BY AID OF
TAIL

The top feather is always in the centre of the tail, whilst the remainder take their positions beneath one another, thus bringing the outer feathers to the bottom.

NOTE.—Recollection of this fact makes the closed tail of a bird very simple to understand, and will avoid a very common mistake found in drawings of the tail being inserted upside down.

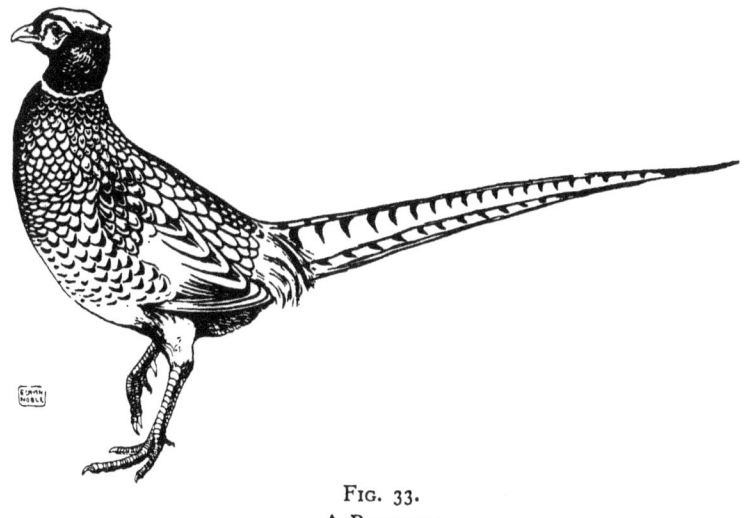

FIG. 33.
A PHEASANT

Although the shape of a bird's tail will vary considerably, the number of feathers is usually the same, namely, twelve.

The Wild Duck, however, has sixteen, but the four extra feathers which are in the centre are different in colour and turn upwards, forming the sickle shapes so characteristic of these birds.

The Humming Bird is again an exception, having only seven feathers, whilst the abnormal Fantail Pigeon has developed nearly forty tail feathers.

NOTE.—When drawing birds, particular notice should be taken of the characteristic manner in which some species use their tails to express their emotions. The Blackbird upon

PLATE XXXIX

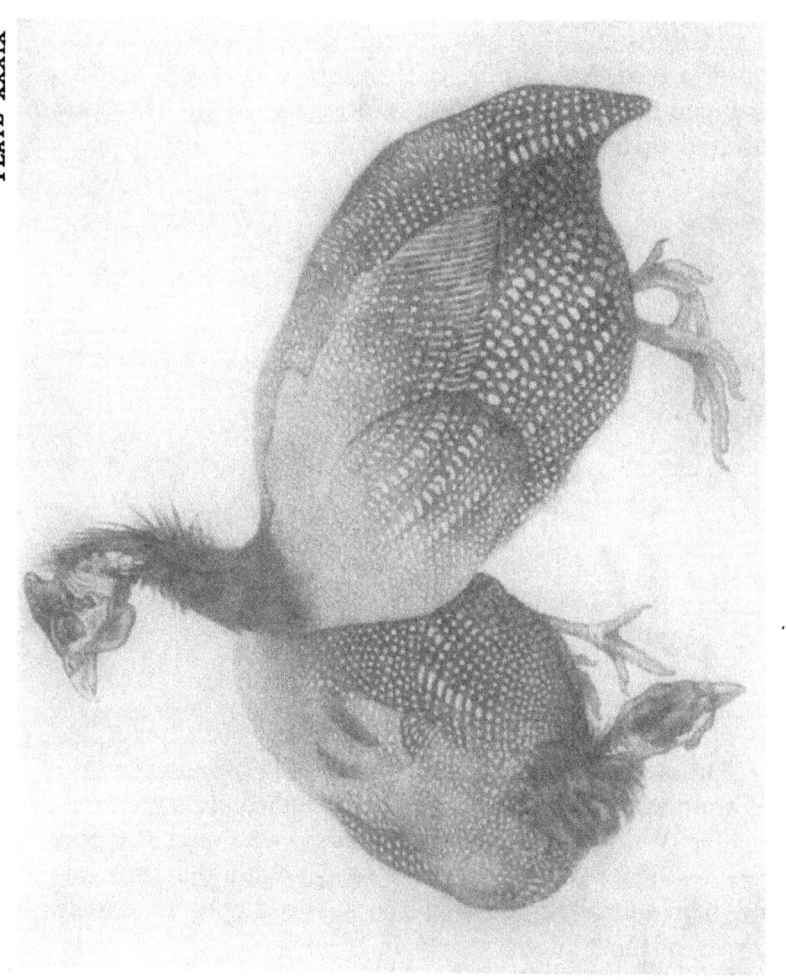

STUDY OF A GUINEA FOWL
SHOWING PATTERN ON PLUMAGE

PLATE XL

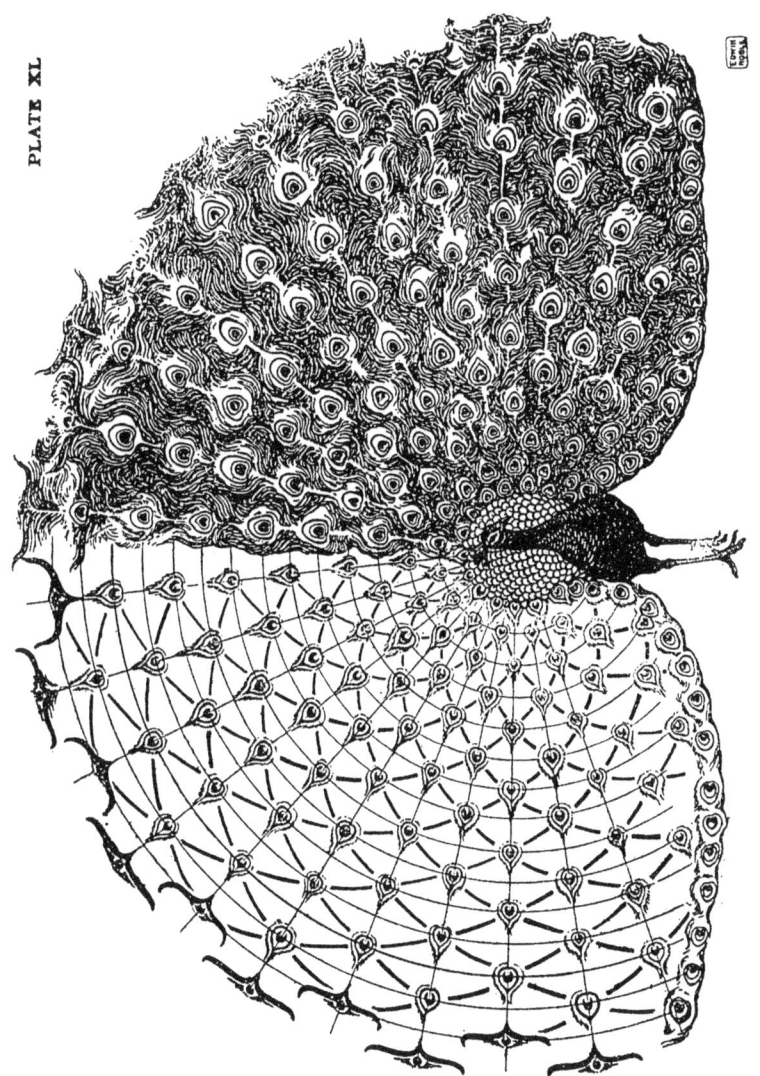

STUDY OF A PEACOCK
SHOWING PATTERN OF THE TAIL

alighting, carries the tail high for a few seconds, in a totally different manner to that when hopping along the ground.

The general rule is that quiet, soft mannered birds hold the tail low and beneath the wing tips, whilst energetic and inquisitive birds, such as the Wren, carry it erect.

At the base of the true tail feathers will be found a series of smaller feathers on both upper and lower sides of the tail, known as the tail coverts, and in certain birds they play an important part in forming sham tails.

The statement that the arrangement of tail feathers has no exception will probably be queried when consideration is given to the tail of the domestic cock.   In this bird, however, the real tail consists of short, stiff feathers of dingy hue, arranged to form a roof-shaped wedge, and serves as a support for the beautiful sickle feathers which are actually Upper Tail Coverts.

In all respects, with the exception of the head, the general rule of feather masses applies to the domestic Fowl, and a similar arrangement can be plainly observed when that magnificent bird, the Turkey Cock is in full display.   The Pheasant, again, is obedient to the same law, although small variations in some of the details will be observed.

The Peacock is so essentially a bird of decoration and offers such a wide scope for variety of treatment, that this book would be incomplete without a diagram showing the tail outspread (Plate xl).

Whilst in no way desirous to hamper the imaginative treatment or convention of the designer, who, after all, is justified in making his own laws, it is quite possible to treat this bird in a perfectly decorative manner and yet be scientifically correct.

The tail proper of the Peacock consists of twelve grey stiff feathers, hidden by and supporting the decorative tail, which is actually the coverts and feathers of the back. The wings are never visible in front of the tail when the latter is outspread.

CHAPTER VI

WILD ANIMALS

IT is sometimes said, second thoughts are best, but applied to the sketching of wild animals they may become an error of judgment. It is of such paramount importance that the mental and visual impression received by the first glimpse of an unfamiliar animal should be retained; it being the fountain from which, perhaps, the source of inspiration may flow at a later date. Our first view of a Giraffe may be that of a dappled shape against the sun-splashed foliage, and the vision is a delicate pattern of cream, fawn, and green; or it may be a glance inside a building and an impression received of a gaunt, towering caricature of the animal world. Neither of these instantaneous glances or impressions should be dismissed from the mind, but stored in the memory for future reference, perhaps to be revived many years later in the form of a vivid character study. This is the art of visualisation, and should be part of the training of every young student. It can be acquired with practice, and no finer method can be devised of demonstrating the importance of essentials such as action, pose, proportions and character, and the secondary position of mere details. The correct number of tail feathers or the exactness of the stripes has an interest in the final result, but is negligible in comparison with the importance of the characterisation.

When drawing from the Giraffe (Plate XLI) note the prominence of the shoulders and the sloping back. The apparent knock-knee aspect of the forelegs and the grotesque hindquarters, the articulations of the spinal column

PLATE XLI

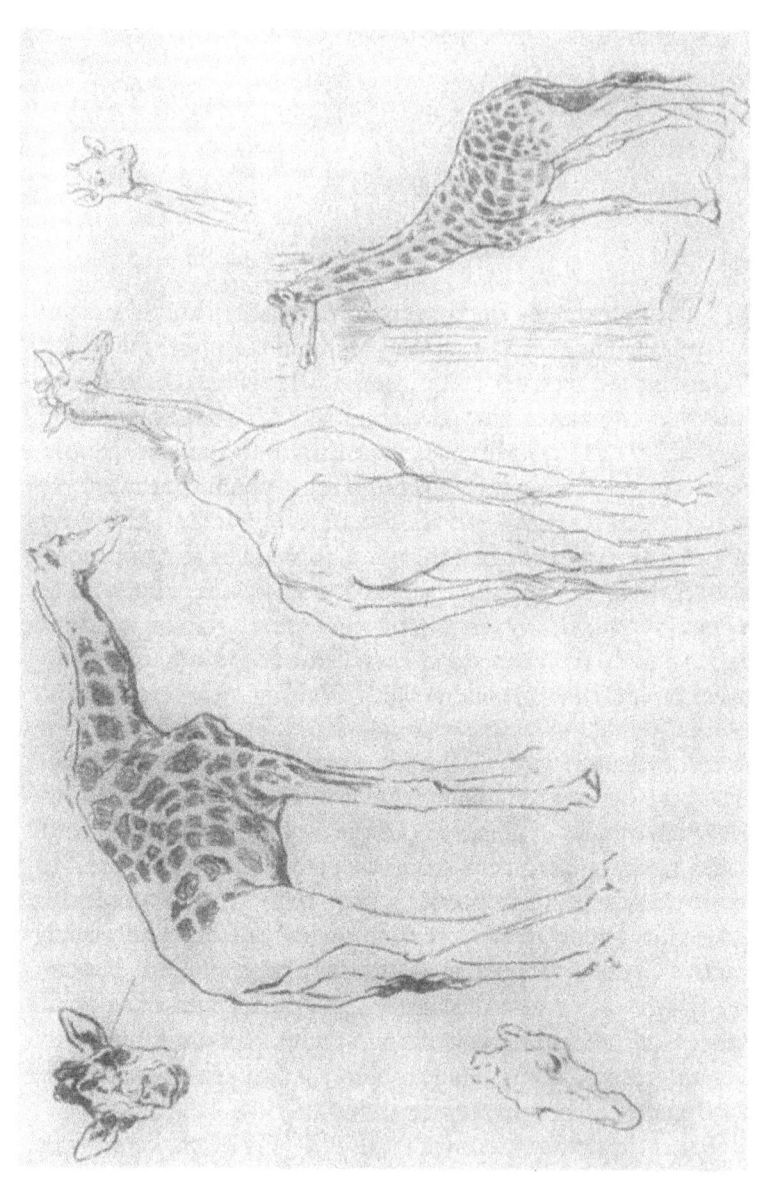

88

PLATE XLII

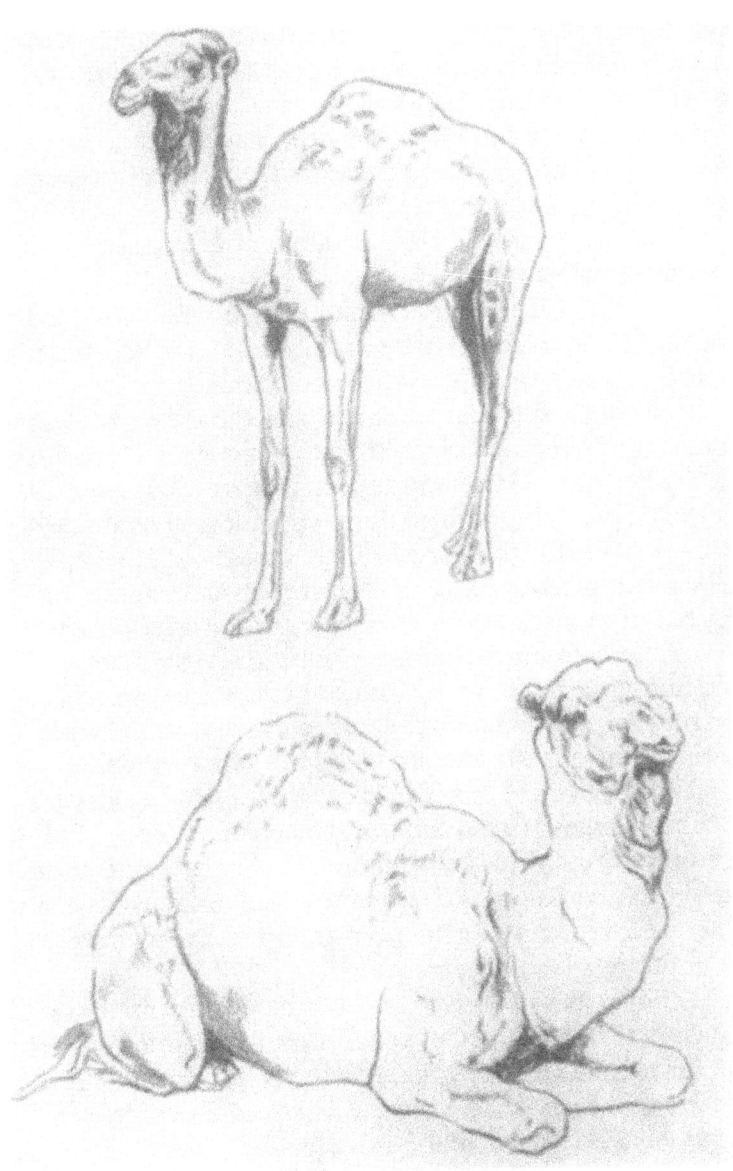

STUDY OF CAMELS

in the neck, and particularly the facial expression. In this respect the Giraffe is, perhaps, one of the exceptions which prove the general rule, for it is not the ears and tail, but the mobile lips and limpid eyes which enable it to demonstrate so effectively the supercilious smile, the bucolic joker, or the melancholic dyspeptic.

Artistically, the Giraffe is a failure, but an excellent test of draughtsmanship.

The Camel (Plate XLII) is another good model for the student. Its movements are not hurried and it will often stand in the same position for long periods.

Again, both this animal and the Giraffe are excellent training on account of their size. It demands a breadth and largeness of observation to put correctly upon a small sheet of paper the proportions of an animal several times the height of the observer. This faculty applies with equal truthfulness to other models such as trees and buildings, but in these cases a point of view can usually be selected for the purpose, whereas with animals the choice is often not with the artist. Upon one occasion I was obliged to observe my model through a keyhole and more than once from a precarious perch upon the top of a step-ladder.

Kangaroos (Plate XLIII) are, again, excellent practice for the cultivation of a broad and free method of drawing. They pose quietly and with an infinite variety of graceful positions. Confusion of pattern and coloration is almost absent and full use should be made of them to develop and improve a feeble technique.

The Polar Bear (Plate XLIV), as a model, appeals to all the instincts of the artist, equalled, perhaps, but not greater than those called forth by the drawing of the human figure. The most delicate of handling is required to contrast the firm bony structure of the head with the massive and yet subtle lines of the fur-covered body. The exact moment when to draw is essential. Its poses, so dignified and statuesque in themselves, are not always suitable for the

PLATE XLIII

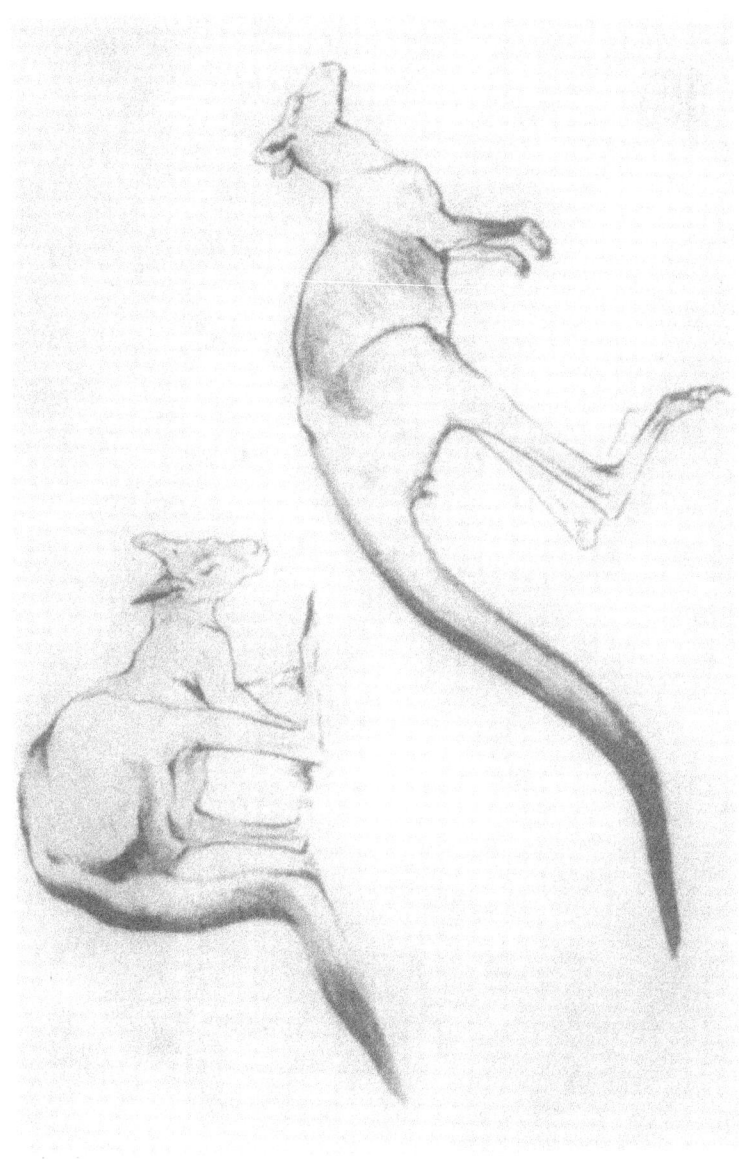

STUDY OF KANGAROOS

PLATE XLIV

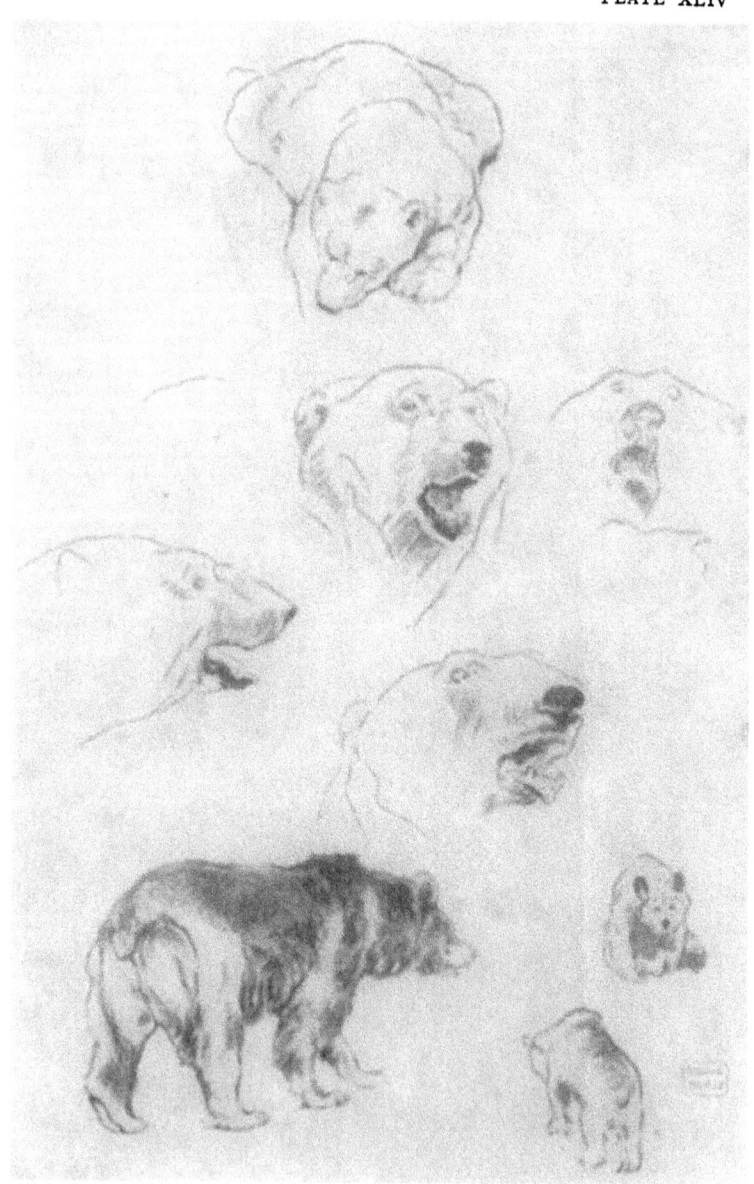

STUDY OF BEARS

PLATE XLV

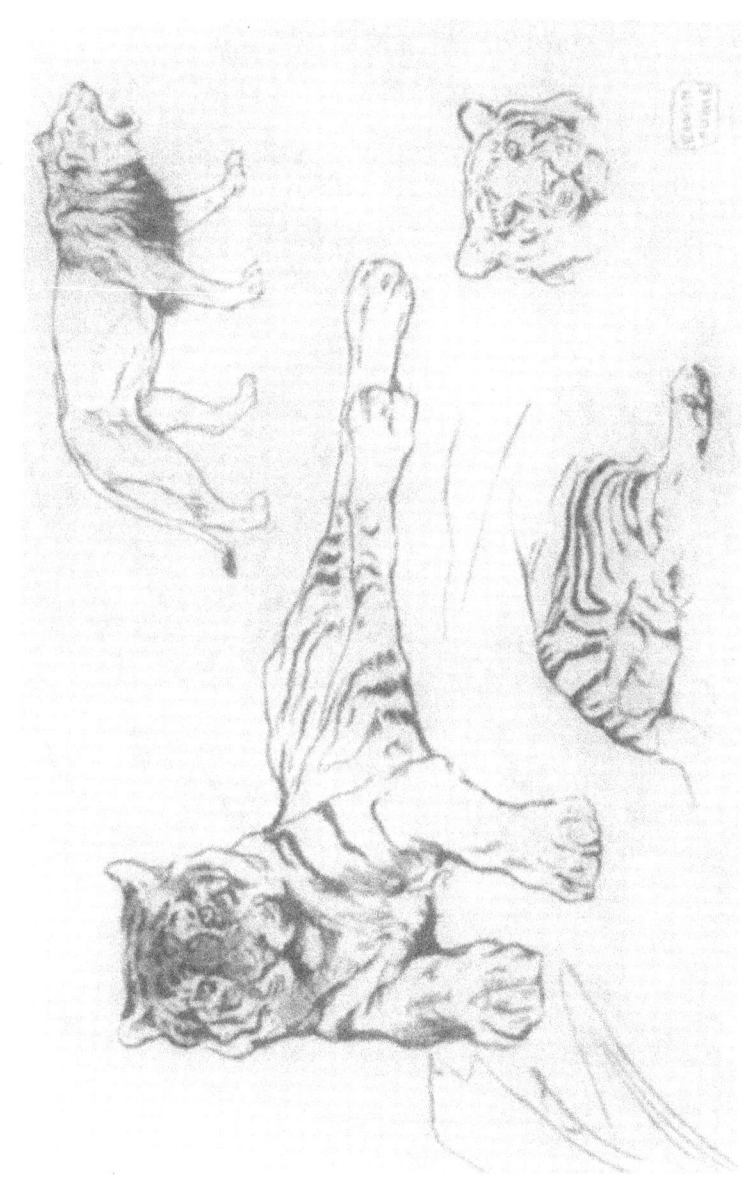

93

pencil, and hours of watchfulness may be required to put down in a few simple strokes all the concentrated strength and beauty of the beast.

The Brown Bear (Plate XLIV), on the contrary, is merely a study of hair and possesses little of interest to the artist apart from its hold upon the affections of the general public.

Drawings of interest can always be obtained from Lions, Lionesses, Tigers, Leopards, etc. Every method of

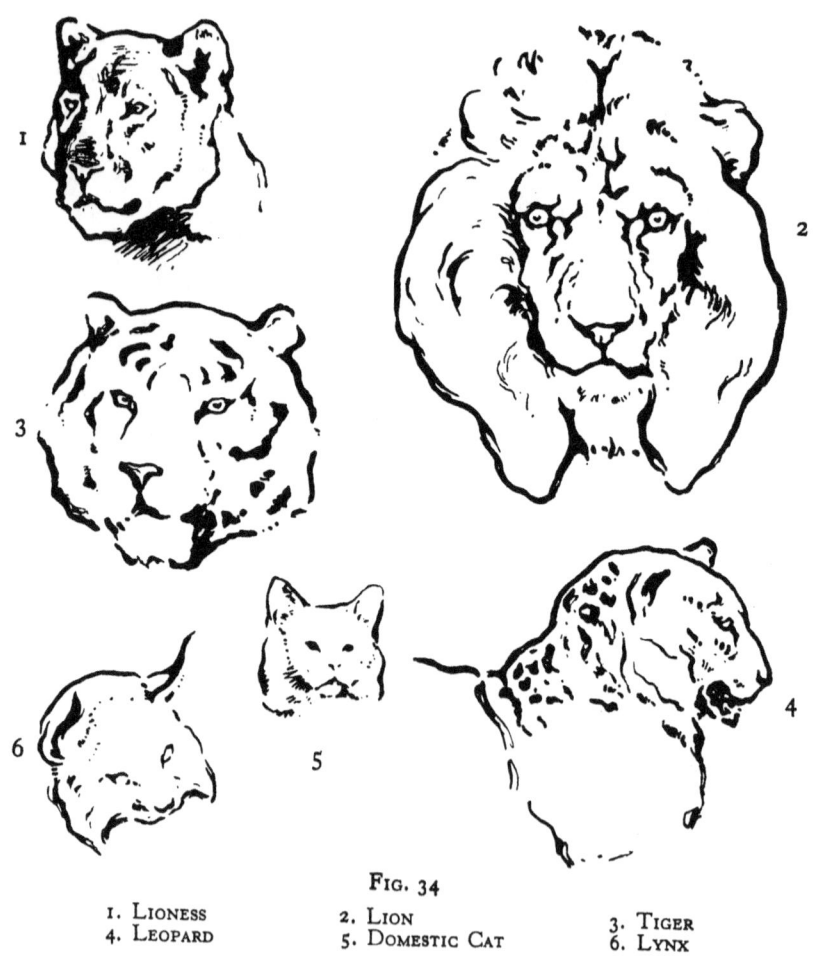

FIG. 34

1. LIONESS	2. LION	3. TIGER
4. LEOPARD	5. DOMESTIC CAT	6. LYNX

PLATE XLVI

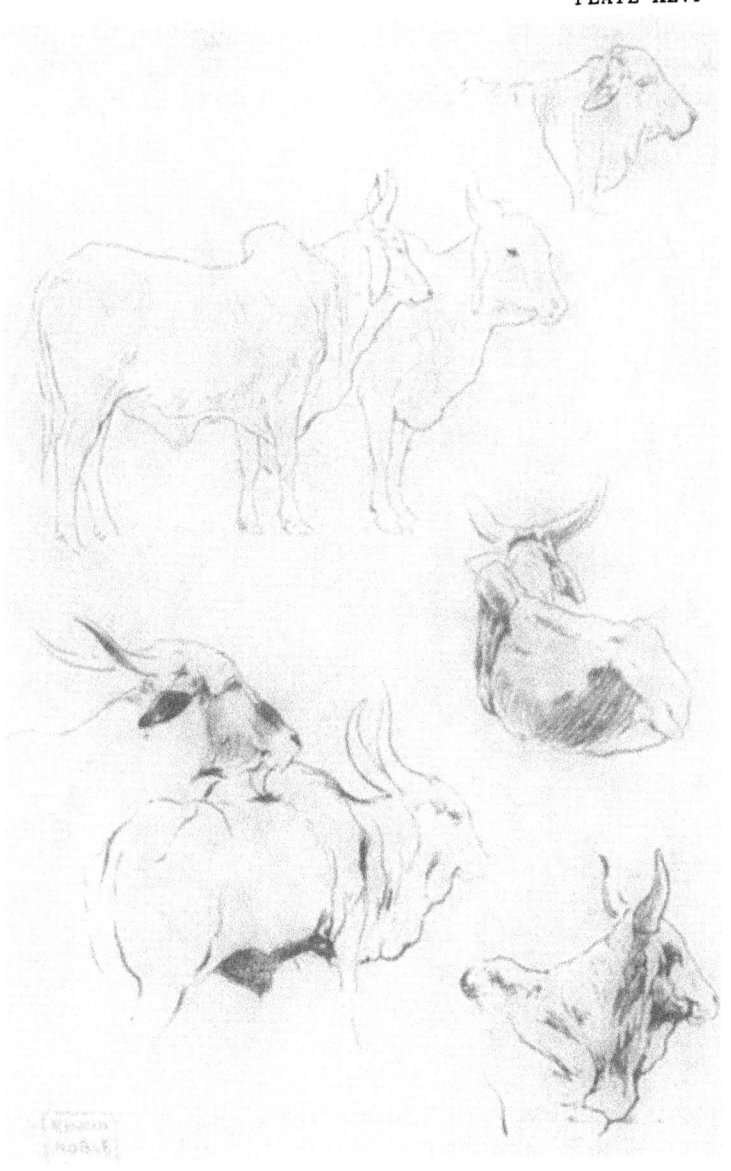

STUDY OF INDIAN CATTLE

technique can be employed, and varying from the purely
decorative to the naturalistic.   The broadside view of a
Lion yawning (Plate XLV) is an example of a vivid, quick

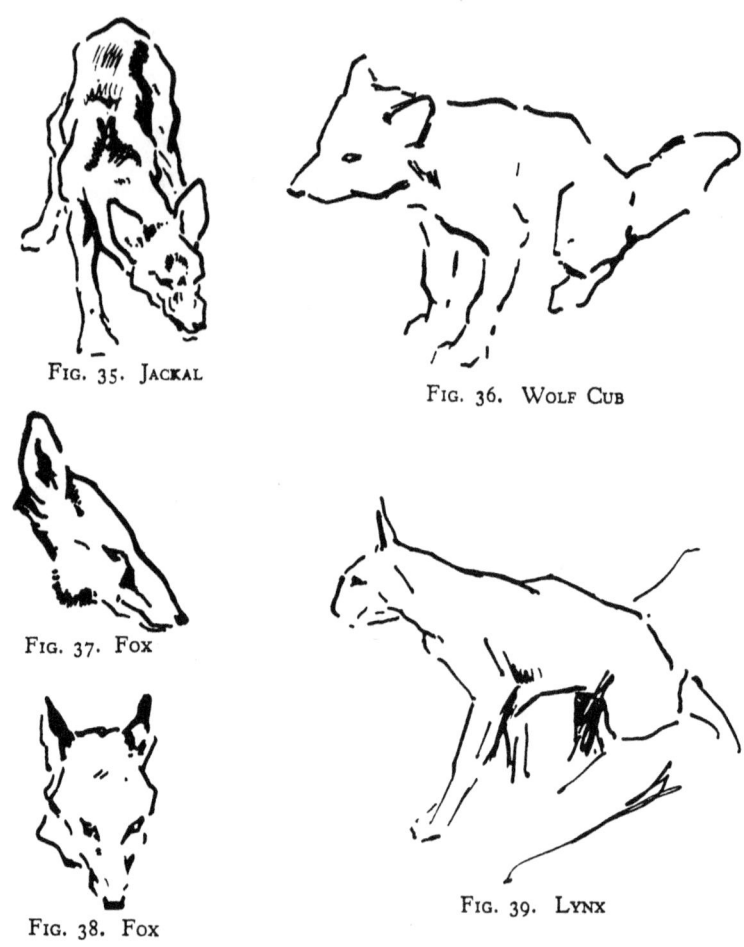

FIG. 35. JACKAL

FIG. 36.   WOLF CUB

FIG. 37. FOX

FIG. 38. FOX

FIG. 39.   LYNX

sketch elaborated by continued study. Although, perhaps,
the final result is not so artistically satisfying as the broader
treatment of the Polar Bear, it is shown as an example of
the results which should be easily obtained by a young
student.

PLATE XLVII

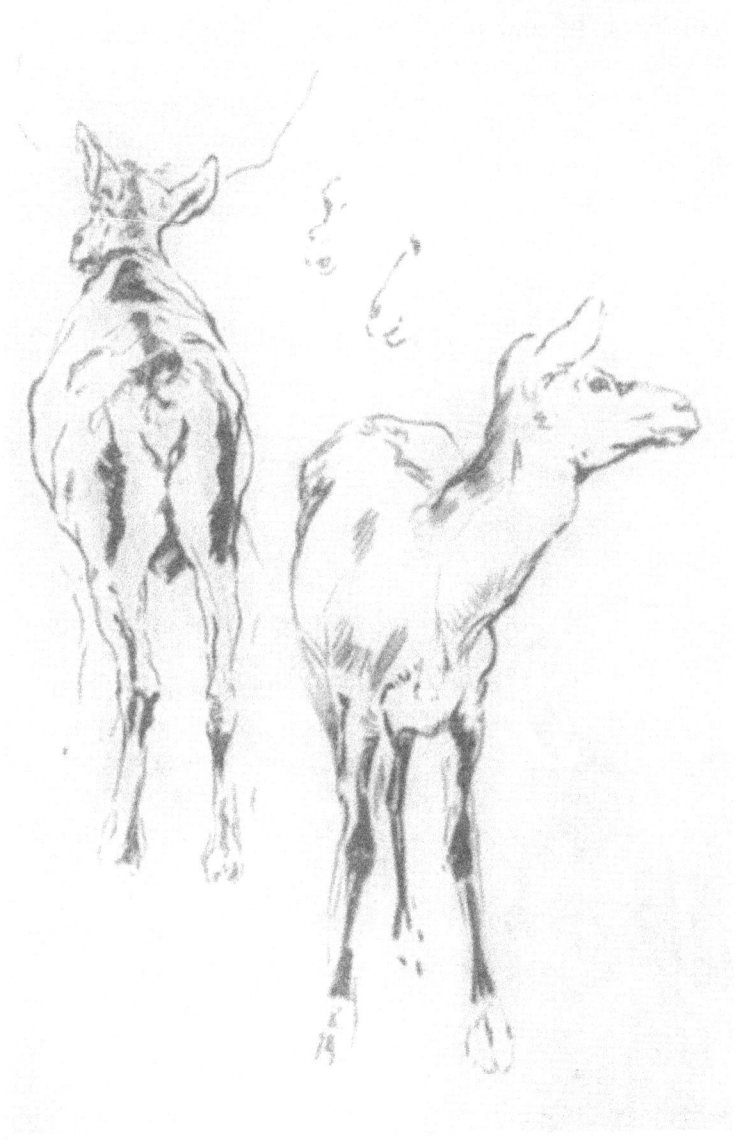

STUDY OF WAPITI

Professor Arthur Thomson, in his book, " The Art
Anatomy of Animals," has shown most concisely the
arrangement and growth of the hair forming the mane of
the Lion, and every student should familiarise themselves
with this diagram. Further to this, note should be
made of the development of hair upon the jaws of the cat
tribe and its importance to the artist. Upon the head of the

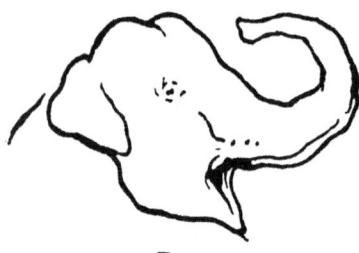

FIG. 40

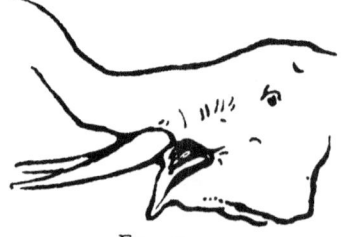

FIG. 41

Tiger very little of the
striping has been intro-
duced, and yet the distinct
character is quite obvious.
This growth is also present
upon the domestic cat and,
carried further, upon the
Lynx, finally forming al-
most a halo upon the head
of the Lion.

It has been previously
stated in this book that
efforts should always be
made to avoid the stuffed
animal appearance, and
that a suggestion of the
twitching tail or move-
ments of the ears will give
the touch of life. A perfect

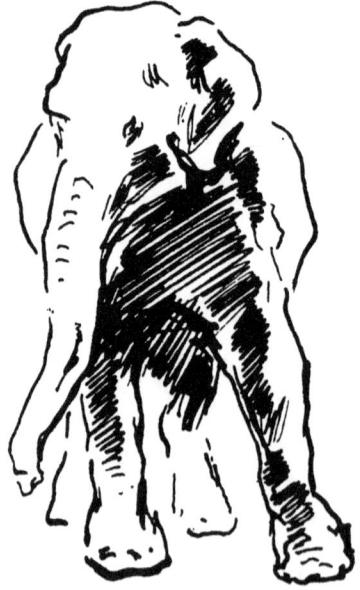

FIG. 42
FRONT VIEW OF ELEPHANT

PLATE XLVIII

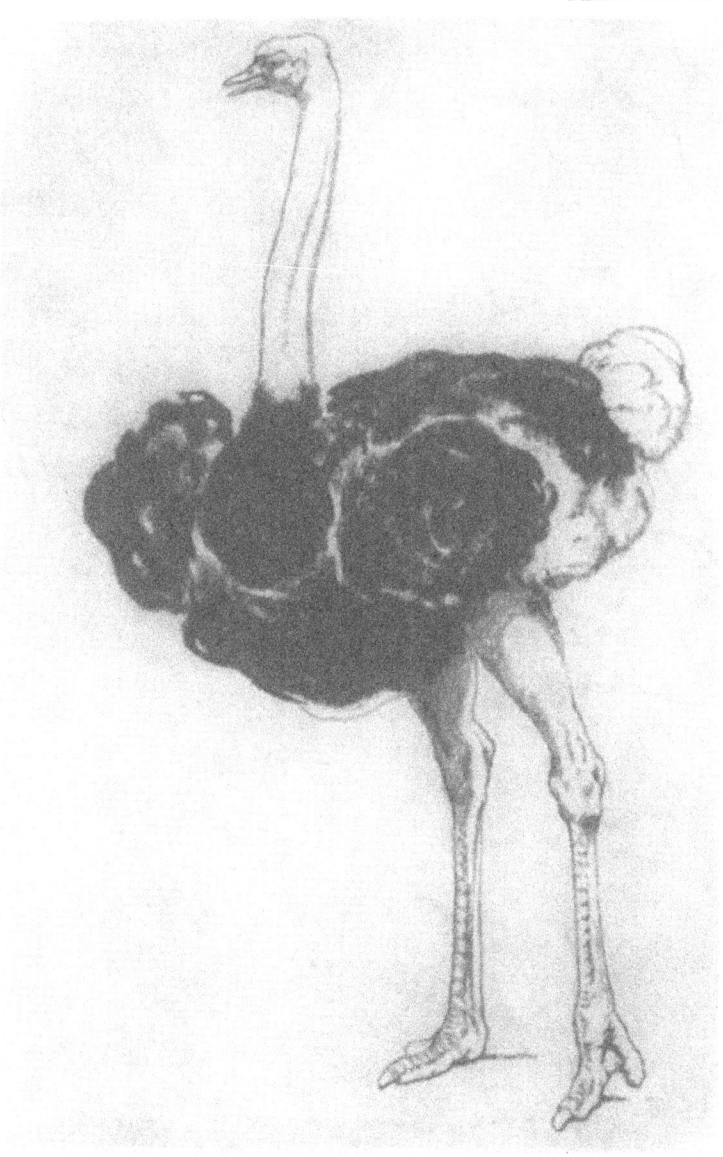

STUDY OF AN OSTRICH

PLATE XLIX

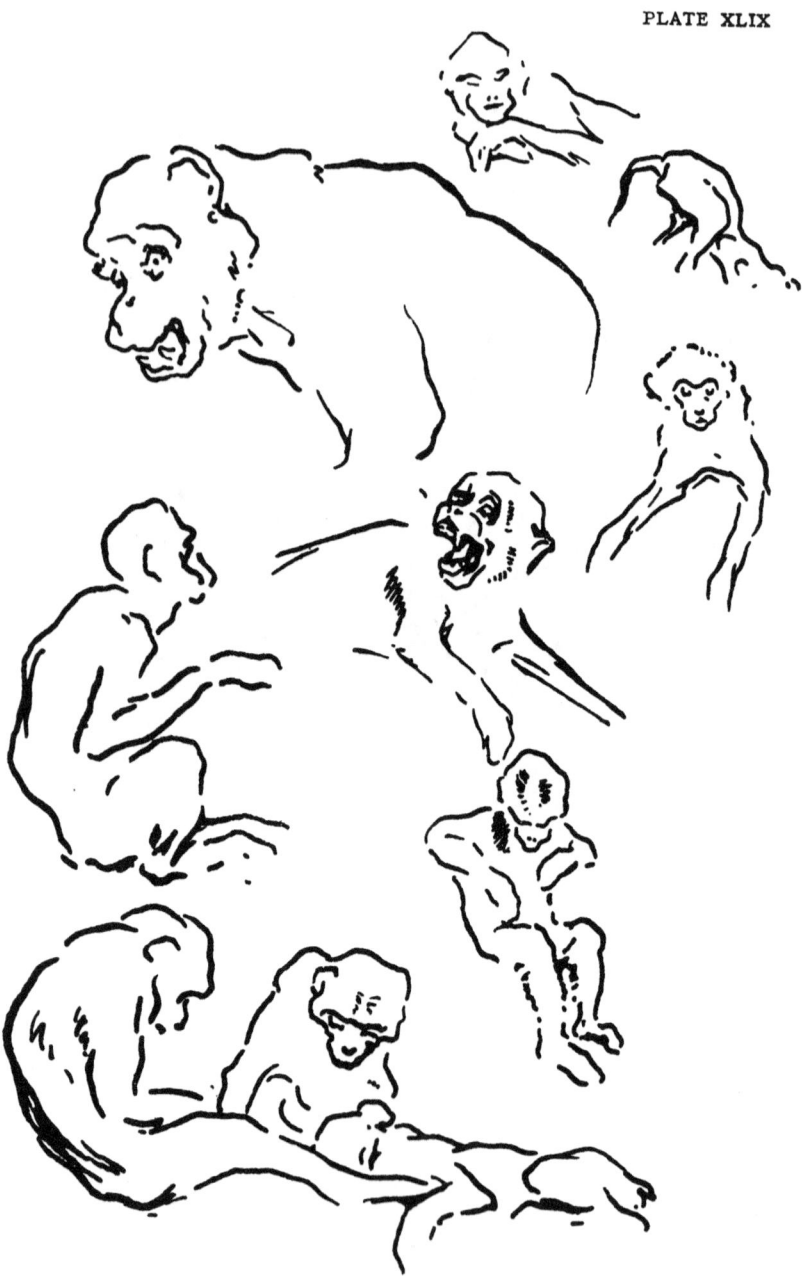

"ACTION" STUDIES OF MONKEYS

example of such details will be found in the decorative drawing of an Ostrich with its raised foot and turn of the head.

This bird also makes an excellent example for a lesson upon evolution. The wings have almost disappeared, and are no longer of use as aids to flight, having neither primary nor secondary feathers. The Ostrich relies for safety upon its fleetness of foot, and when running at full speed will use the wings in a rotary or windmill action to help its progress. The foot bears a close resemblance to that of the Horse, the hoof being represented by the big toe nail, whilst the remaining toe ceases to perform any useful function.

The remaining plates should be of interest to a student, inasmuch as they are pages reproduced direct from a sketchbook and introduced in order to show a variety of technique. The daintiness and grace of the Indian Cattle (Plate XLVI) obviously required the most delicate handling of the pencil, with a loving patience which will enable the exquisite modelling to be captured.

Plate XLVII. The front foreshortened view of a Wapiti is an interesting contrast. A momentary pause, when both brain and pencil must move at lightning speed to capture the arrested action, requires a simplification of technique, and this may be observed in the suggestiveness of the treatment of the slender forelegs. As a sketch, the rear view of the same animal is not quite so successful, the head being rather heavy and laboured. A slighter treatment of this detail would have helped the impression of foreshortening.

For drawings such as these, my own preference is to use a carbon pencil upon smooth paper. A twist of the fingers will give either a broad flat point or one of copperplate fineness, whilst greater or less pressure to accentuate a colour or detail becomes almost automatic. Sketching direct in pen and ink has never appealed to me, owing to the rigid inflexibility of the pen point, but I admit that many splendid results have been achieved in this method. When used, however, it is, perhaps, advisable to accentuate slightly the angles, and by so doing stress the character, or otherwise the solid black of the ink is apt to make the outlines become rather monotonous. For examples, note the head of the young Fox (Fig. 38) and also the Lynx (Fig. 39).

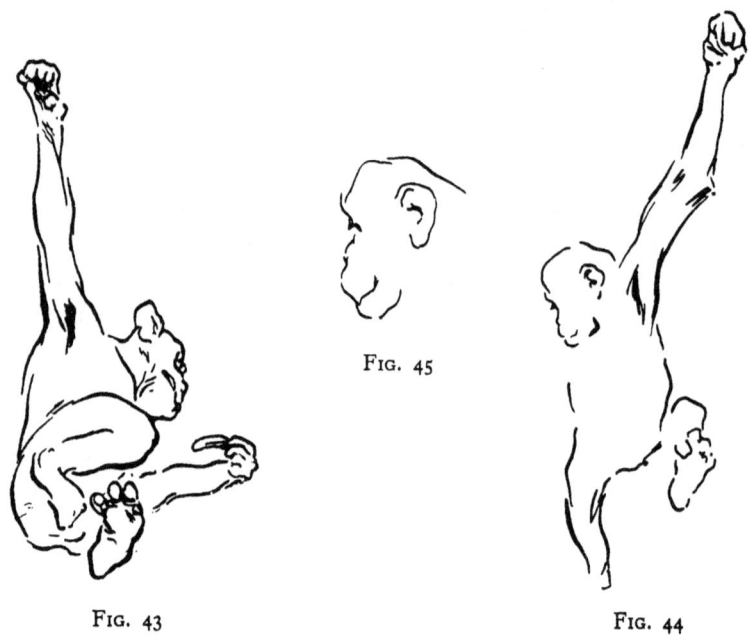

FIG. 45

FIG. 43

FIG. 44

As quick sketches (Fig. 36) Wolf Cub, and (Fig. 35) Jackal, are interesting, but nothing more. There is not sufficient material to work from at any future date, and the same criticism may be applied to the page of Monkeys (Plate XLIX). The studies of Chimpanzees have, however, far more valuable qualities of suggestion, and the quick foreshortened sketch of an Elephant (Fig. 42) has captured the elusive action of this huge beast as he rocks from side to side and transfers his weight from leg to leg. As an example of observation, this drawing is, perhaps, unequalled throughout this book.

Animal painting to-day is woefully neglected, and perhaps this is not to be wondered at when the difficulties are considered. The varieties of animals alone amount to some hundreds, each having its own zoological or anatomical peculiarity, and a thorough knowledge of this is necessary before elimination of unessentials is begun. The artist has, however, the art of selection, that priceless gift which enables him to rise above the camera and the film. The true picture appeals more by what is left unsaid than by facts given.

INDEX

INDEX—(continued)

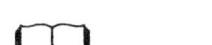

A CATALOG OF SELECTED DOVER BOOKS IN ALL FIELDS OF INTEREST

100 BEST-LOVED POEMS, Edited by Philip Smith. "The Passionate Shepherd to His Love," "Shall I compare thee to a summer's day?" "Death, be not proud," "The Raven," "The Road Not Taken," plus works by Blake, Wordsworth, Byron, Shelley, Keats, many others. 96pp. $5\frac{3}{16}$ x $8\frac{1}{4}$. 0-486-28553-7

100 SMALL HOUSES OF THE THIRTIES, Brown-Blodgett Company. Exterior photographs and floor plans for 100 charming structures. Illustrations of models accompanied by descriptions of interiors, color schemes, closet space, and other amenities. 200 illustrations. 112pp. $8\frac{3}{8}$ x 11. 0-486-44131-8

1000 TURN-OF-THE-CENTURY HOUSES: With Illustrations and Floor Plans, Herbert C. Chivers. Reproduced from a rare edition, this showcase of homes ranges from cottages and bungalows to sprawling mansions. Each house is meticulously illustrated and accompanied by complete floor plans. 256pp. $9\frac{3}{8}$ x $12\frac{1}{4}$. 0-486-45596-3

101 GREAT AMERICAN POEMS, Edited by The American Poetry & Literacy Project. Rich treasury of verse from the 19th and 20th centuries includes works by Edgar Allan Poe, Robert Frost, Walt Whitman, Langston Hughes, Emily Dickinson, T. S. Eliot, other notables. 96pp. $5\frac{3}{16}$ x $8\frac{1}{4}$. 0-486-40158-8

101 GREAT SAMURAI PRINTS, Utagawa Kuniyoshi. Kuniyoshi was a master of the warrior woodblock print — and these 18th-century illustrations represent the pinnacle of his craft. Full-color portraits of renowned Japanese samurais pulse with movement, passion, and remarkably fine detail. 112pp. $8\frac{3}{8}$ x 11. 0-486-46523-3

ABC OF BALLET, Janet Grosser. Clearly worded, abundantly illustrated little guide defines basic ballet-related terms: arabesque, battement, pas de chat, relevé, sissonne, many others. Pronunciation guide included. Excellent primer. 48pp. $4\frac{3}{16}$ x $5\frac{3}{4}$. 0-486-40871-X

ACCESSORIES OF DRESS: An Illustrated Encyclopedia, Katherine Lester and Bess Viola Oerke. Illustrations of hats, veils, wigs, cravats, shawls, shoes, gloves, and other accessories enhance an engaging commentary that reveals the humor and charm of the many-sided story of accessorized apparel. 644 figures and 59 plates. 608pp. 6 $\frac{1}{8}$ x $9\frac{1}{4}$. 0-486-43378-1

ADVENTURES OF HUCKLEBERRY FINN, Mark Twain. Join Huck and Jim as their boyhood adventures along the Mississippi River lead them into a world of excitement, danger, and self-discovery. Humorous narrative, lyrical descriptions of the Mississippi valley, and memorable characters. 224pp. $5\frac{3}{16}$ x $8\frac{1}{4}$. 0-486-28061-6

ALICE STARMORE'S BOOK OF FAIR ISLE KNITTING, Alice Starmore. A noted designer from the region of Scotland's Fair Isle explores the history and techniques of this distinctive, stranded-color knitting style and provides copious illustrated instructions for 14 original knitwear designs. 208pp. $8\frac{3}{8}$ x $10\frac{7}{8}$. 0-486-47218-3

Browse over 9,000 books at www.doverpublications.com

ALICE'S ADVENTURES IN WONDERLAND, Lewis Carroll. Beloved classic about a little girl lost in a topsy-turvy land and her encounters with the White Rabbit, March Hare, Mad Hatter, Cheshire Cat, and other delightfully improbable characters. 42 illustrations by Sir John Tenniel. 96pp. 5³⁄₁₆ x 8¼. 0-486-27543-4

AMERICA'S LIGHTHOUSES: An Illustrated History, Francis Ross Holland. Profusely illustrated fact-filled survey of American lighthouses since 1716. Over 200 stations — East, Gulf, and West coasts, Great Lakes, Hawaii, Alaska, Puerto Rico, the Virgin Islands, and the Mississippi and St. Lawrence Rivers. 240pp. 8 x 10¾.
0-486-25576-X

AN ENCYCLOPEDIA OF THE VIOLIN, Alberto Bachmann. Translated by Frederick H. Martens. Introduction by Eugene Ysaye. First published in 1925, this renowned reference remains unsurpassed as a source of essential information, from construction and evolution to repertoire and technique. Includes a glossary and 73 illustrations. 496pp. 6⅛ x 9¼. 0-486-46618-3

ANIMALS: 1,419 Copyright-Free Illustrations of Mammals, Birds, Fish, Insects, etc., Selected by Jim Harter. Selected for its visual impact and ease of use, this outstanding collection of wood engravings presents over 1,000 species of animals in extremely lifelike poses. Includes mammals, birds, reptiles, amphibians, fish, insects, and other invertebrates. 284pp. 9 x 12. 0-486-23766-4

THE ANNALS, Tacitus. Translated by Alfred John Church and William Jackson Brodribb. This vital chronicle of Imperial Rome, written by the era's great historian, spans A.D. 14-68 and paints incisive psychological portraits of major figures, from Tiberius to Nero. 416pp. 5³⁄₁₆ x 8¼. 0-486-45236-0

ANTIGONE, Sophocles. Filled with passionate speeches and sensitive probing of moral and philosophical issues, this powerful and often-performed Greek drama reveals the grim fate that befalls the children of Oedipus. Footnotes. 64pp. 5³⁄₁₆ x 8 ¼. 0-486-27804-2

ART DECO DECORATIVE PATTERNS IN FULL COLOR, Christian Stoll. Reprinted from a rare 1910 portfolio, 160 sensuous and exotic images depict a breathtaking array of florals, geometrics, and abstracts — all elegant in their stark simplicity. 64pp. 8⅜ x 11. 0-486-44862-2

THE ARTHUR RACKHAM TREASURY: 86 Full-Color Illustrations, Arthur Rackham. Selected and Edited by Jeff A. Menges. A stunning treasury of 86 full-page plates span the famed English artist's career, from *Rip Van Winkle* (1905) to masterworks such as *Undine, A Midsummer Night's Dream,* and *Wind in the Willows* (1939). 96pp. 8⅜ x 11.
0-486-44685-9

THE AUTHENTIC GILBERT & SULLIVAN SONGBOOK, W. S. Gilbert and A. S. Sullivan. The most comprehensive collection available, this songbook includes selections from every one of Gilbert and Sullivan's light operas. Ninety-two numbers are presented uncut and unedited, and in their original keys. 410pp. 9 x 12.
0-486-23482-7

THE AWAKENING, Kate Chopin. First published in 1899, this controversial novel of a New Orleans wife's search for love outside a stifling marriage shocked readers. Today, it remains a first-rate narrative with superb characterization. New introductory Note. 128pp. 5³⁄₁₆ x 8¼. 0-486-27786-0

BASIC DRAWING, Louis Priscilla. Beginning with perspective, this commonsense manual progresses to the figure in movement, light and shade, anatomy, drapery, composition, trees and landscape, and outdoor sketching. Black-and-white illustrations throughout. 128pp. 8⅜ x 11. 0-486-45815-6

THE BATTLES THAT CHANGED HISTORY, Fletcher Pratt. Historian profiles 16 crucial conflicts, ancient to modern, that changed the course of Western civilization. Gripping accounts of battles led by Alexander the Great, Joan of Arc, Ulysses S. Grant, other commanders. 27 maps. 352pp. 5⅜ x 8½. 0-486-41129-X

BEETHOVEN'S LETTERS, Ludwig van Beethoven. Edited by Dr. A. C. Kalischer. Features 457 letters to fellow musicians, friends, greats, patrons, and literary men. Reveals musical thoughts, quirks of personality, insights, and daily events. Includes 15 plates. 410pp. 5⅜ x 8½. 0-486-22769-3

BERNICE BOBS HER HAIR AND OTHER STORIES, F. Scott Fitzgerald. This brilliant anthology includes 6 of Fitzgerald's most popular stories: "The Diamond as Big as the Ritz," the title tale, "The Offshore Pirate," "The Ice Palace," "The Jelly Bean," and "May Day." 176pp. 5⅜ x 8½. 0-486-47049-0

BESLER'S BOOK OF FLOWERS AND PLANTS: 73 Full-Color Plates from Hortus Eystettensis, 1613, Basilius Besler. Here is a selection of magnificent plates from the *Hortus Eystettensis*, which vividly illustrated and identified the plants, flowers, and trees that thrived in the legendary German garden at Eichstätt. 80pp. 8⅜ x 11. 0-486-46005-3

THE BOOK OF KELLS, Edited by Blanche Cirker. Painstakingly reproduced from a rare facsimile edition, this volume contains full-page decorations, portraits, illustrations, plus a sampling of textual leaves with exquisite calligraphy and ornamentation. 32 full-color illustrations. 32pp. 9⅜ x 12¼. 0-486-24345-1

THE BOOK OF THE CROSSBOW: With an Additional Section on Catapults and Other Siege Engines, Ralph Payne-Gallwey. Fascinating study traces history and use of crossbow as military and sporting weapon, from Middle Ages to modern times. Also covers related weapons: balistas, catapults, Turkish bows, more. Over 240 illustrations. 400pp. 7¼ x 10⅛. 0-486-28720-3

THE BUNGALOW BOOK: Floor Plans and Photos of 112 Houses, 1910, Henry L. Wilson. Here are 112 of the most popular and economic blueprints of the early 20th century — plus an illustration or photograph of each completed house. A wonderful time capsule that still offers a wealth of valuable insights. 160pp. 8⅜ x 11. 0-486-45104-6

THE CALL OF THE WILD, Jack London. A classic novel of adventure, drawn from London's own experiences as a Klondike adventurer, relating the story of a heroic dog caught in the brutal life of the Alaska Gold Rush. Note. 64pp. 5³⁄₁₆ x 8¼. 0-486-26472-6

CANDIDE, Voltaire. Edited by Francois-Marie Arouet. One of the world's great satires since its first publication in 1759. Witty, caustic skewering of romance, science, philosophy, religion, government — nearly all human ideals and institutions. 112pp. 5³⁄₁₆ x 8¼. 0-486-26689-3

CELEBRATED IN THEIR TIME: Photographic Portraits from the George Grantham Bain Collection, Edited by Amy Pastan. With an Introduction by Michael Carlebach. Remarkable portrait gallery features 112 rare images of Albert Einstein, Charlie Chaplin, the Wright Brothers, Henry Ford, and other luminaries from the worlds of politics, art, entertainment, and industry. 128pp. 8⅜ x 11. 0-486-46754-6

CHARIOTS FOR APOLLO: The NASA History of Manned Lunar Spacecraft to 1969, Courtney G. Brooks, James M. Grimwood, and Loyd S. Swenson, Jr. This illustrated history by a trio of experts is the definitive reference on the Apollo spacecraft and lunar modules. It traces the vehicles' design, development, and operation in space. More than 100 photographs and illustrations. 576pp. 6¾ x 9¼. 0-486-46756-2

A CHRISTMAS CAROL, Charles Dickens. This engrossing tale relates Ebenezer Scrooge's ghostly journeys through Christmases past, present, and future and his ultimate transformation from a harsh and grasping old miser to a charitable and compassionate human being. 80pp. 5¾₆ x 8¼. 0-486-26865-9

COMMON SENSE, Thomas Paine. First published in January of 1776, this highly influential landmark document clearly and persuasively argued for American separation from Great Britain and paved the way for the Declaration of Independence. 64pp. 5¾₆ x 8¼. 0-486-29602-4

THE COMPLETE SHORT STORIES OF OSCAR WILDE, Oscar Wilde. Complete texts of "The Happy Prince and Other Tales," "A House of Pomegranates," "Lord Arthur Savile's Crime and Other Stories," "Poems in Prose," and "The Portrait of Mr. W. H." 208pp. 5¾₆ x 8¼. 0-486-45216-6

COMPLETE SONNETS, William Shakespeare. Over 150 exquisite poems deal with love, friendship, the tyranny of time, beauty's evanescence, death, and other themes in language of remarkable power, precision, and beauty. Glossary of archaic terms. 80pp. 5¾₆ x 8¼. 0-486-26686-9

THE COUNT OF MONTE CRISTO: Abridged Edition, Alexandre Dumas. Falsely accused of treason, Edmond Dantès is imprisoned in the bleak Chateau d'If. After a hair-raising escape, he launches an elaborate plot to extract a bitter revenge against those who betrayed him. 448pp. 5¾₆ x 8¼. 0-486-45643-9

CRAFTSMAN BUNGALOWS: Designs from the Pacific Northwest, Yoho & Merritt. This reprint of a rare catalog, showcasing the charming simplicity and cozy style of Craftsman bungalows, is filled with photos of completed homes, plus floor plans and estimated costs. An indispensable resource for architects, historians, and illustrators. 112pp. 10 x 7. 0-486-46875-5

CRAFTSMAN BUNGALOWS: 59 Homes from "The Craftsman," Edited by Gustav Stickley. Best and most attractive designs from Arts and Crafts Movement publication — 1903–1916 — includes sketches, photographs of homes, floor plans, descriptive text. 128pp. 8¼ x 11. 0-486-25829-7

CRIME AND PUNISHMENT, Fyodor Dostoyevsky. Translated by Constance Garnett. Supreme masterpiece tells the story of Raskolnikov, a student tormented by his own thoughts after he murders an old woman. Overwhelmed by guilt and terror, he confesses and goes to prison. 480pp. 5¾₆ x 8¼. 0-486-41587-2

THE DECLARATION OF INDEPENDENCE AND OTHER GREAT DOCUMENTS OF AMERICAN HISTORY: 1775-1865, Edited by John Grafton. Thirteen compelling and influential documents: Henry's "Give Me Liberty or Give Me Death," Declaration of Independence, The Constitution, Washington's First Inaugural Address, The Monroe Doctrine, The Emancipation Proclamation, Gettysburg Address, more. 64pp. 5¾₆ x 8¼. 0-486-41124-9

THE DESERT AND THE SOWN: Travels in Palestine and Syria, Gertrude Bell. "The female Lawrence of Arabia," Gertrude Bell wrote captivating, perceptive accounts of her travels in the Middle East. This intriguing narrative, accompanied by 160 photos, traces her 1905 sojourn in Lebanon, Syria, and Palestine. 368pp. 5⅜ x 8½. 0-486-46876-3

A DOLL'S HOUSE, Henrik Ibsen. Ibsen's best-known play displays his genius for realistic prose drama. An expression of women's rights, the play climaxes when the central character, Nora, rejects a smothering marriage and life in "a doll's house." 80pp. 5¾₆ x 8¼. 0-486-27062-9

DOOMED SHIPS: Great Ocean Liner Disasters, William H. Miller, Jr. Nearly 200 photographs, many from private collections, highlight tales of some of the vessels whose pleasure cruises ended in catastrophe: the *Morro Castle, Normandie, Andrea Doria, Europa,* and many others. 128pp. 8⅞ x 11¼. 0-486-45366-9

THE DORÉ BIBLE ILLUSTRATIONS, Gustave Doré. Detailed plates from the Bible: the Creation scenes, Adam and Eve, horrifying visions of the Flood, the battle sequences with their monumental crowds, depictions of the life of Jesus, 241 plates in all. 241pp. 9 x 12. 0-486-23004-X

DRAWING DRAPERY FROM HEAD TO TOE, Cliff Young. Expert guidance on how to draw shirts, pants, skirts, gloves, hats, and coats on the human figure, including folds in relation to the body, pull and crush, action folds, creases, more. Over 200 drawings. 48pp. 8¼ x 11. 0-486-45591-2

DUBLINERS, James Joyce. A fine and accessible introduction to the work of one of the 20th century's most influential writers, this collection features 15 tales, including a masterpiece of the short-story genre, "The Dead." 160pp. 5³⁄₁₆ x 8¼. 0-486-26870-5

EASY-TO-MAKE POP-UPS, Joan Irvine. Illustrated by Barbara Reid. Dozens of wonderful ideas for three-dimensional paper fun — from holiday greeting cards with moving parts to a pop-up menagerie. Easy-to-follow, illustrated instructions for more than 30 projects. 299 black-and-white illustrations. 96pp. 8⅜ x 11. 0-486-44622-0

EASY-TO-MAKE STORYBOOK DOLLS: A "Novel" Approach to Cloth Dollmaking, Sherralyn St. Clair. Favorite fictional characters come alive in this unique beginner's dollmaking guide. Includes patterns for Pollyanna, Dorothy from *The Wonderful Wizard of Oz,* Mary of *The Secret Garden,* plus easy-to-follow instructions, 263 black-and-white illustrations, and an 8-page color insert. 112pp. 8¼ x 11. 0-486-47360-0

EINSTEIN'S ESSAYS IN SCIENCE, Albert Einstein. Speeches and essays in accessible, everyday language profile influential physicists such as Niels Bohr and Isaac Newton. They also explore areas of physics to which the author made major contributions. 128pp. 5 x 8. 0-486-47011-3

EL DORADO: Further Adventures of the Scarlet Pimpernel, Baroness Orczy. A popular sequel to *The Scarlet Pimpernel,* this suspenseful story recounts the Pimpernel's attempts to rescue the Dauphin from imprisonment during the French Revolution. An irresistible blend of intrigue, period detail, and vibrant characterizations. 352pp. 5³⁄₁₆ x 8¼. 0-486-44026-5

ELEGANT SMALL HOMES OF THE TWENTIES: 99 Designs from a Competition, Chicago Tribune. Nearly 100 designs for five- and six-room houses feature New England and Southern colonials, Normandy cottages, stately Italianate dwellings, and other fascinating snapshots of American domestic architecture of the 1920s. 112pp. 9 x 12. 0-486-46910-7

THE ELEMENTS OF STYLE: The Original Edition, William Strunk, Jr. This is the book that generations of writers have relied upon for timeless advice on grammar, diction, syntax, and other essentials. In concise terms, it identifies the principal requirements of proper style and common errors. 64pp. 5⅜ x 8½. 0-486-44798-7

THE ELUSIVE PIMPERNEL, Baroness Orczy. Robespierre's revolutionaries find their wicked schemes thwarted by the heroic Pimpernel — Sir Percival Blakeney. In this thrilling sequel, Chauvelin devises a plot to eliminate the Pimpernel and his wife. 272pp. 5³⁄₁₆ x 8¼. 0-486-45464-9

Browse over 9,000 books at www.doverpublications.com

AN ENCYCLOPEDIA OF BATTLES: Accounts of Over 1,560 Battles from 1479 B.C. to the Present, David Eggenberger. Essential details of every major battle in recorded history from the first battle of Megiddo in 1479 B.C. to Grenada in 1984. List of battle maps. 99 illustrations. 544pp. 6½ x 9¼. 0-486-24913-1

ENCYCLOPEDIA OF EMBROIDERY STITCHES, INCLUDING CREWEL, Marion Nichols. Precise explanations and instructions, clearly illustrated, on how to work chain, back, cross, knotted, woven stitches, and many more — 178 in all, including Cable Outline, Whipped Satin, and Eyelet Buttonhole. Over 1400 illustrations. 219pp. 8⅜ x 11¼. 0-486-22929-7

ENTER JEEVES: 15 Early Stories, P. G. Wodehouse. Splendid collection contains first 8 stories featuring Bertie Wooster, the deliciously dim aristocrat and Jeeves, his brainy, imperturbable manservant. Also, the complete Reggie Pepper (Bertie's prototype) series. 288pp. 5⅜ x 8½. 0-486-29717-9

ERIC SLOANE'S AMERICA: Paintings in Oil, Michael Wigley. With a Foreword by Mimi Sloane. Eric Sloane's evocative oils of America's landscape and material culture shimmer with immense historical and nostalgic appeal. This original hardcover collection gathers nearly a hundred of his finest paintings, with subjects ranging from New England to the American Southwest. 128pp. 10⅝ x 9. 0-486-46525-X

ETHAN FROME, Edith Wharton. Classic story of wasted lives, set against a bleak New England background. Superbly delineated characters in a hauntingly grim tale of thwarted love. Considered by many to be Wharton's masterpiece. 96pp. 5³⁄₁₆ x 8 ¼. 0-486-26690-7

THE EVERLASTING MAN, G. K. Chesterton. Chesterton's view of Christianity — as a blend of philosophy and mythology, satisfying intellect and spirit — applies to his brilliant book, which appeals to readers' heads as well as their hearts. 288pp. 5⅜ x 8½. 0-486-46036-3

THE FIELD AND FOREST HANDY BOOK, Daniel Beard. Written by a co-founder of the Boy Scouts, this appealing guide offers illustrated instructions for building kites, birdhouses, boats, igloos, and other fun projects, plus numerous helpful tips for campers. 448pp. 5³⁄₁₆ x 8¼. 0-486-46191-2

FINDING YOUR WAY WITHOUT MAP OR COMPASS, Harold Gatty. Useful, instructive manual shows would-be explorers, hikers, bikers, scouts, sailors, and survivalists how to find their way outdoors by observing animals, weather patterns, shifting sands, and other elements of nature. 288pp. 5⅜ x 8½. 0-486-40613-X

FIRST FRENCH READER: A Beginner's Dual-Language Book, Edited and Translated by Stanley Appelbaum. This anthology introduces 50 legendary writers — Voltaire, Balzac, Baudelaire, Proust, more — through passages from *The Red and the Black, Les Misérables, Madame Bovary,* and other classics. Original French text plus English translation on facing pages. 240pp. 5⅜ x 8½. 0-486-46178-5

FIRST GERMAN READER: A Beginner's Dual-Language Book, Edited by Harry Steinhauer. Specially chosen for their power to evoke German life and culture, these short, simple readings include poems, stories, essays, and anecdotes by Goethe, Hesse, Heine, Schiller, and others. 224pp. 5⅜ x 8½. 0-486-46179-3

FIRST SPANISH READER: A Beginner's Dual-Language Book, Angel Flores. Delightful stories, other material based on works of Don Juan Manuel, Luis Taboada, Ricardo Palma, other noted writers. Complete faithful English translations on facing pages. Exercises. 176pp. 5⅜ x 8½. 0-486-25810-6

Browse over 9,000 books at www.doverpublications.com

FIVE ACRES AND INDEPENDENCE, Maurice G. Kains. Great back-to-the-land classic explains basics of self-sufficient farming. The one book to get. 95 illustrations. 397pp. 5⅜ x 8½. 0-486-20974-1

FLAGG'S SMALL HOUSES: Their Economic Design and Construction, 1922, Ernest Flagg. Although most famous for his skyscrapers, Flagg was also a proponent of the well-designed single-family dwelling. His classic treatise features innovations that save space, materials, and cost. 526 illustrations. 160pp. 9⅜ x 12¼.
0-486-45197-6

FLATLAND: A Romance of Many Dimensions, Edwin A. Abbott. Classic of science (and mathematical) fiction — charmingly illustrated by the author — describes the adventures of A. Square, a resident of Flatland, in Spaceland (three dimensions), Lineland (one dimension), and Pointland (no dimensions). 96pp. 5³⁄₁₆ x 8¼.
0-486-27263-X

FRANKENSTEIN, Mary Shelley. The story of Victor Frankenstein's monstrous creation and the havoc it caused has enthralled generations of readers and inspired countless writers of horror and suspense. With the author's own 1831 introduction. 176pp. 5³⁄₁₆ x 8¼. 0-486-28211-2

THE GARGOYLE BOOK: 572 Examples from Gothic Architecture, Lester Burbank Bridaham. Dispelling the conventional wisdom that French Gothic architectural flourishes were born of despair or gloom, Bridaham reveals the whimsical nature of these creations and the ingenious artisans who made them. 572 illustrations. 224pp. 8⅜ x 11. 0-486-44754-5

THE GIFT OF THE MAGI AND OTHER SHORT STORIES, O. Henry. Sixteen captivating stories by one of America's most popular storytellers. Included are such classics as "The Gift of the Magi," "The Last Leaf," and "The Ransom of Red Chief." Publisher's Note. 96pp. 5³⁄₁₆ x 8¼. 0-486-27061-0

THE GOETHE TREASURY: Selected Prose and Poetry, Johann Wolfgang von Goethe. Edited, Selected, and with an Introduction by Thomas Mann. In addition to his lyric poetry, Goethe wrote travel sketches, autobiographical studies, essays, letters, and proverbs in rhyme and prose. This collection presents outstanding examples from each genre. 368pp. 5⅜ x 8½. 0-486-44780-4

GREAT EXPECTATIONS, Charles Dickens. Orphaned Pip is apprenticed to the dirty work of the forge but dreams of becoming a gentleman — and one day finds himself in possession of "great expectations." Dickens' finest novel. 400pp. 5³⁄₁₆ x 8¼.
0-486-41586-4

GREAT WRITERS ON THE ART OF FICTION: From Mark Twain to Joyce Carol Oates, Edited by James Daley. An indispensable source of advice and inspiration, this anthology features essays by Henry James, Kate Chopin, Willa Cather, Sinclair Lewis, Jack London, Raymond Chandler, Raymond Carver, Eudora Welty, and Kurt Vonnegut, Jr. 192pp. 5⅜ x 8½. 0-486-45128-3

HAMLET, William Shakespeare. The quintessential Shakespearean tragedy, whose highly charged confrontations and anguished soliloquies probe depths of human feeling rarely sounded in any art. Reprinted from an authoritative British edition complete with illuminating footnotes. 128pp. 5³⁄₁₆ x 8¼. 0-486-27278-8

THE HAUNTED HOUSE, Charles Dickens. A Yuletide gathering in an eerie country retreat provides the backdrop for Dickens and his friends — including Elizabeth Gaskell and Wilkie Collins — who take turns spinning supernatural yarns. 144pp. 5⅜ x 8½. 0-486-46309-5

Browse over 9,000 books at www.doverpublications.com

HEART OF DARKNESS, Joseph Conrad. Dark allegory of a journey up the Congo River and the narrator's encounter with the mysterious Mr. Kurtz. Masterly blend of adventure, character study, psychological penetration. For many, Conrad's finest, most enigmatic story. 80pp. 5³⁄₁₆ x 8¼. 0-486-26464-5

HENSON AT THE NORTH POLE, Matthew A. Henson. This thrilling memoir by the heroic African-American who was Peary's companion through two decades of Arctic exploration recounts a tale of danger, courage, and determination. "Fascinating and exciting." — *Commonweal.* 128pp. 5⅜ x 8½. 0-486-45472-X

HISTORIC COSTUMES AND HOW TO MAKE THEM, Mary Fernald and E. Shenton. Practical, informative guidebook shows how to create everything from short tunics worn by Saxon men in the fifth century to a lady's bustle dress of the late 1800s. 81 illustrations. 176pp. 5⅜ x 8½. 0-486-44906-8

THE HOUND OF THE BASKERVILLES, Arthur Conan Doyle. A deadly curse in the form of a legendary ferocious beast continues to claim its victims from the Baskerville family until Holmes and Watson intervene. Often called the best detective story ever written. 128pp. 5³⁄₁₆ x 8¼. 0-486-28214-7

THE HOUSE BEHIND THE CEDARS, Charles W. Chesnutt. Originally published in 1900, this groundbreaking novel by a distinguished African-American author recounts the drama of a brother and sister who "pass for white" during the dangerous days of Reconstruction. 208pp. 5⅜ x 8½. 0-486-46144-0

THE HUMAN FIGURE IN MOTION, Eadweard Muybridge. The 4,789 photographs in this definitive selection show the human figure — models almost all undraped — engaged in over 160 different types of action: running, climbing stairs, etc. 390pp. 7⅞ x 10⅝. 0-486-20204-6

THE IMPORTANCE OF BEING EARNEST, Oscar Wilde. Wilde's witty and buoyant comedy of manners, filled with some of literature's most famous epigrams, reprinted from an authoritative British edition. Considered Wilde's most perfect work. 64pp. 5³⁄₁₆ x 8¼. 0-486-26478-5

THE INFERNO, Dante Alighieri. Translated and with notes by Henry Wadsworth Longfellow. The first stop on Dante's famous journey from Hell to Purgatory to Paradise, this 14th-century allegorical poem blends vivid and shocking imagery with graceful lyricism. Translated by the beloved 19th-century poet, Henry Wadsworth Longfellow. 256pp. 5³⁄₁₆ x 8¼. 0-486-44288-8

JANE EYRE, Charlotte Brontë. Written in 1847, *Jane Eyre* tells the tale of an orphan girl's progress from the custody of cruel relatives to an oppressive boarding school and its culmination in a troubled career as a governess. 448pp. 5³⁄₁₆ x 8¼. 0-486-42449-9

JAPANESE WOODBLOCK FLOWER PRINTS, Tanigami Kônan. Extraordinary collection of Japanese woodblock prints by a well-known artist features 120 plates in brilliant color. Realistic images from a rare edition include daffodils, tulips, and other familiar and unusual flowers. 128pp. 11 x 8¼. 0-486-46442-3

JEWELRY MAKING AND DESIGN, Augustus F. Rose and Antonio Cirino. Professional secrets of jewelry making are revealed in a thorough, practical guide. Over 200 illustrations. 306pp. 5⅜ x 8½. 0-486-21750-7

JULIUS CAESAR, William Shakespeare. Great tragedy based on Plutarch's account of the lives of Brutus, Julius Caesar and Mark Antony. Evil plotting, ringing oratory, high tragedy with Shakespeare's incomparable insight, dramatic power. Explanatory footnotes. 96pp. 5³⁄₁₆ x 8¼. 0-486-26876-4

Browse over 9,000 books at www.doverpublications.com